BRIGHAM YOUNG
UNIVERSITY
IDAHO

Donated By: J. Michael Shires

on behalf of Dr. George Wood

D1572315

Days of Freedom:
A Coeur d'Alene Boyhood

Published in 2002
by Tornado Creek Publications
Printed in the United States of America
by
Walsworth Publishing Company
Marceline, Missouri

ISBN (hardbound) 0-9652219-8-9
Pacific Northwesterner version ISSN 0030-882X

Cover photo: George Wood with his dog Prince.

Tornado Creek Publications
Tony and Suzanne Bamonte
P.O. Box 8625
Spokane, Washington 99203-8625
(509) 838-7114

Days of Freedom:
A Coeur d'Alene
Boyhood

by

George E. Wood

Tornado Creek Publications
Spokane, Washington 2002

Editor's Note: Personal Memoirs as History

Many people in the leisure of retirement write memoirs of their early years for the enjoyment and enlightenment of their families and to pass on to future generations. Often illustrated with family photos, they provide an intimate record of the childhood of an individual and the life of a family. A few of these memoirs serve a larger purpose, however: they provide a lens through which to view a specific period in the history of a town or region. When they are as well written and rich in detail as the narrative published in this expanded issue of *Pacific Northwesterner,* they can make a significant contribution to regional and social history.

George Wood grew up in Coeur d'Alene during a period when small-town life retained a bustle and vitality, yet simplicity and safety, which have largely disappeared from the American scene. George was free to roam his world, and his range was considerable: the town, with its streets and shops; the waterfront, with its sawmills and docks, where the last of the steamboats still called; the lake, with its vast opportunities for fishing, boating, camping and enjoying the family cabin; and the forest, largely a wilderness of huge trees, where logging still depended upon the brawn of men and horses. George was allowed a freedom unheard of for children of the present day to explore this fascinating environment.

Coeur d'Alene was not just any town. Because of its location and variety, it was an exceptionally interesting place. It was a hub for lumber, mining, and transportation. By means of interurban rail, one could get to the "big city" of Spokane. Its setting was, and is, exceptionally beautiful. Yet it was also a microcosm of small-town life throughout the United States. With its churches, schools, saloons, barbershops, new movie theaters, telephones and cars, its doctors, lawyers, laborers, its club ladies and lodge men, its reformers and its hooligans, it could be "everytown." The sharp eye and ear of the young George Wood caught this life and he remembered it well.

Even as a family memoir, this narrative provides more social history than is typical. The Wood family was unusual in its level of civic involvement and status in the community. George's father, a prominent doctor and Coeur d'Alene's mayor for a time, was involved in most aspects of the town's life. George's active, intelligent mother was far more then a typical housewife. Their large, lovely home was the setting of family meals, much pleasant social life and community cultural activity. George Wood grew up loved, yet firmly instructed and disciplined within this secure environment, and his narrative provides a picture of the sort of family life that, unfortunately, is now more the exception than the rule.

As Westerners know, history is not all facts, figures and famous people. It can also be the life experiences of people like ourselves who spent their formative years in the Inland Northwest.

Laura Arksey

This book is dedicated with love to my three grandsons: Michael Shires, Craig Shires and Eric Jacobson.

George Wood

George Wood, high school graduation, 1935.

George Wood was born May 29, 1918 in Coeur d'Alene, Idaho, to Dr. John T. and Margaret (Thomson) Wood. He attended local public schools and graduated from Coeur d'Alene High School in 1935. His higher education was at Eastern Washington University, University of Idaho and the University of Minnesota, where he received a D.D.S. in 1942. He was a dentist in the Army Air Corps from 1942 to 1946. In 1947 he received a graduate degree in Pediatric Dentistry at the University of California and practiced in Spokane from 1948 until his retirement in 1985. He established the dental care program for Spokane's Headstart Program and was president of the Spokane Dental Society and the Washington Dental Service Corporation. He is a charter member of the Exchange Club in Spokane. He married Jean Fischer in 1943 and they have three daughters, Chris Ann Gain, Caroline Law and Carla Wood. His interests are sculpture, music, art, photography and, above all, history, about which he does considerable writing. He wrote a newsletter for the Museum of North Idaho and currently has a manuscript forthcoming on the early history of Coeur d'Alene and the Wood and Thomson families.

Carefree adventures with my best friend, Eddie McManniman, left. This photo is from the summer I spent in the logging camps with Eddie and his father.

The early years of my life were truly "days of freedom." We could go where we wanted and do what we wanted without too much danger. We did have a few restrictions, but they were the ones imposed by how things had always been done. We did not have dangers from drugs, guns and social upheavals. There might have been a small amount of religious conflict, but it revolved around whether one went to the Catholic school or the public schools. All summer long and on weekends we all played together and were friends. With ready access to the lakes, hills and forests, it was an idyllic setting for growing boys. We were not paragons of virtue and some of our escapades led to danger, but the dangers were largely of our own making, unlike those faced by young boys today.

The Coeur d'Alene of my boyhood was a fascinating little town which was in a transitional phase. The little settlement had grown around Fort Sherman, which had been established in 1878 to protect the whites from the Indians in the region. The fort was on a point which jutted out into the lake at the mouth of the Spokane River, and the town was oriented to the lake from its first days. It evolved into an inland port city, with railroads, boats, a brewery and summer excursionists. In 1918 when I was born the fort was gone, the brewery had closed because of Prohibition and much of the boat traffic had ceased. The city depended on lumber mills and summer tourists for its economic survival.

There were still big boats on the lake and people who depended on them for transportation of themselves and their household goods. There were still passenger trains for travel to Spokane. The Great Northern had electric passenger trains from Spokane to Coeur d'Alene and also out to Hayden Lake. The Northern Pacific carried passengers from Spokane on a train pulled by a steam locomotive which crossed Sherman Avenue right in the middle of town on Third Street. Both of these railroads also hauled freight as did the Milwaukee and the Spokane International. Much of the freight these companies hauled were logs which were dumped into the lake and lumber which was hauled away to the rest of the country.

It was really a lumbering town with the Coeur d'Alene Mill in the center of town, one block from the main intersection. The Rutledge Mill was on the eastern outskirts of town. To the west along the Spokane River, there were three mills, the Blackwell, Winton, and Ohio Match, also some smaller mills and even a box factory.

I was born May 29, 1918 in our home at 1010 Sherman Avenue. My father, Dr. John T. Wood, delivered me. He was the son of English immigrants, William and Sarah Ann (Heaton) Wood, who had come from near Wakefield in the county of Yorkshire to Canada when Dad was eleven. The family later settled in North Dakota, where Dad taught school. In 1905, after completing a medical degree in Detroit, he set up a practice in Coeur d'Alene, which was to continue for his entire career. He was a giant of a man, physically and intellectually, with prodigious energy and strong opinions. In addition to being a busy general practitioner and surgeon, he served as mayor of Coeur d'Alene and later in the United States House of Representatives, his politics swinging from socialist to archconservative in the interval. He was active in many aspects of life in Coeur d'Alene, a Mason and a Rotary president.

My mother, Margaret (Thomson) Wood, was the daughter of a Coeur d'Alene baker, entrepreneur and civic leader, George C. Thomson, and Amelia Melinda (St. Denis) Thomson, who had immigrated from Brockville, Ontario, Canada, to Idaho in 1890. The family had strong Scottish and French Canadian roots. George Thomson was also Grand Master of the Odd Fellows for the state of Idaho. His voluminous diaries chronicle migration from Canada and travels around Idaho for the Odd Fellows. He died in 1906 at age 48, and in 1910 my grandmother married his brother William, a widower. Uncle Bill, as we called him, became one of my cherished relatives and mentors. My parents were married in 1907 when my mother was only sixteen. Before long, she had adapted to the demands of managing the largest house in Coeur d'Alene, providing support for her busy husband, raising her children and contributing to the civic and cultural life of the town.

My father and mother with their 1923 Studebaker in front of our first house at 1010 Sherman Avenue.

It was easy to get to Spokane by interurban train during my childhood. Photo courtesy Leonard Gottschalk.

Sherman Avenue looking west from City Hall.

Thomson's Pavilion in Blackwell Park. My grandfather, George C. Thomson, and Moses Sauve built and operated the pavilion in 1904. They also maintained a bathhouse and rented boats that Sauve built.

I was named after my grandfather Thomson and was the youngest of three children. My sister Dorothy was eight at the time of my birth and my brother William, five. Later that year my sister died in the terrible Spanish influenza epidemic which spread throughout the United States at the end of World War I. My father worked night and day treating the sick, including his own daughter, who was the last person to die in Coeur d'Alene during the epidemic. I suppose because of that tragic loss, I was quite badly spoiled. People said I was a beautiful child and photographs taken of me at that time show me with long curls dressed almost like a little girl.

While growing up I got plenty of attention as my grandmother Thomson and Uncle Bill lived in the second house down the street from ours. As I got older I roamed freely and was welcomed into all the homes in the block, at least that was what I thought. I was kind of the neighborhood pet or maybe pest depending how one might look at it. In my brother's eyes I was definitely a pest.

In my first few years I only remember a smattering of things; one was my dad's radio, probably the first in the city, which was housed in a couple of square boxes with mysterious wires running all over, attached to some big batteries. As it didn't have a speaker, about half a dozen people sat around with earphones plugged into the set listening to stations many miles away. I also remember another one of Dad's hobbies, the cello. He had decided at 39 years of age he wanted to learn to play, so he started taking lessons and really, considering his late start, became quite proficient. There were other disjointed experiences I remember from those years, such as being pulled around in a sled with a box attached to it; going swimming at Sander's Beach; the smell of ether on my dad when he had been operating; and most of all my loving parents.

Another early memory, which somehow is more vivid than others, was the ice wagon. In those years every family had an ice box to keep their food cold and the ice man came around on a routine basis to deliver ice. For some reason, they had not yet begun to use a truck, and the wagon was pulled by a horse. The ice man would cut off a large piece of ice with an ice pick, pick it up with his ice tongs and weigh it with a scale on the back of the wagon. He would then sling it on his back, which was protected from the wet and cold with a heavy leather shield, and carry it into the house where he placed it in the ice box. In the summertime when it was hot, kids would follow the wagon wherever it went, clustering around it looking for chips of ice to eat. That was a real treat!

The milk man also made home deliveries in those days. He would deliver the milk in glass bottles with a swollen portion at the top for the cream and would leave the bottles on people's doorsteps. The cream at the top was thicker than present-day whipping cream.

I suppose you could say I was a mother's boy in my early years before I started to school. My father was so busy with his medicine he didn't have as much time for me as he may have wished. I loved him, but looked up to him in awe. My mother, who was very loving, spent a lot of time reading to me, listening to me and I guess spoiling me. The male influence was supplied by a very loving and patient step-grandfather (Uncle Bill) who was willing to listen. He allowed me to spend time watching while he was working in his shop and guided me in using a few simple tools. I must have been only four or five years old, but he treated me like I was older. To this day I still have very warm feelings for short, plump, white-haired men with mustaches. I wasn't a sissy, however; I got into too much trouble to be placed in that category. Around three I agreed to my brother cutting off my curls. I didn't want them because only girls had curls and I wanted to be a boy. I was happy, but Mother was very unhappy with Bill. I hated to lie down for naps, so I tore a hole in a screen on the sleeping porch and managed to sneak down to Dick Fischer's to play with him. He didn't have to nap.

I was interested in clothes from an early age, even having names for my outfits. This one would be my aviator's suit, this one my sailor suit, and so on, with me giving my mother directions as to what suit I wanted to wear on given days. Age has not changed my fascination with clothes. I am still concerned about my wardrobe. Although I was very fussy about my clothes, I would often get them dirty while playing and my mother would get very disturbed with me. Years later she mentioned one incident when she was taking me somewhere and had already changed me several times that day. I showed up all dirty again and out of exasperation she just dumped me in the tub, clothes and all.

Little boys' clothes were different in my days. I think you could almost divide a boy's pants into stages. As babies we were dressed more like little girls. At two or three we began wearing short pants which were more like the shorts worn nowadays but made of different materials, even velvet. On top we often wore pull-over blouses rather than shirts. Beginning around five or six we started wearing knickers for all dress purposes including going to school. We did wear overalls or levis for play.

Of all pesky creations human beings were ever dressed in, knickers were the worst! In winter when we wore long underwear we first had to pull long stockings over the underwear, keeping one down while the other was pulled up. Then came the knickers which were gathered just below the knee. There were even different styles of knickers. "Plus fours" were still gathered just below the knee but bloused down further. Men golfers even wore what they called plus sixes, but I don't remember that little boys did. I remember my stockings were always lumpy and falling halfway down my legs. The knickers we wore to school were made of a black and white speckled corduroy. For Easter we would get a new suit which usually consisted of a coat, vest and knickers made of a nice wool fabric. With this suit we would wear a shirt and necktie. The rite of manhood came about around eleven or twelve years of age, in junior high school, when we graduated at long last to trousers. That was a memorable experience; we became young men.

The year my parents went back to Chicago was very special for me, because they brought me back a wonderful drum. It was a big wooden one with real hide heads and screws to tighten the head and snares, along with real drum sticks. I was an early riser and I remember

At age three, I was still in curls. Later I donned the hated knick-ers (inset).

getting up every morning at five in my room upstairs on the west side of the house and playing my favorite march, "The American Patrol," on the phonograph as I accompanied it with my drum. Mrs. McCarty next door later told me it didn't bother my parents because they slept on the other side of the house and downstairs. I must not have been their favorite neighbor child.

When I went downtown with my mother we would often be stopped by the train when we reached Third Street. I was intrigued by the huge locomotive that passed just two or three feet from me, moving ponderously with its bell clanging. The wheels towered above me and the drive shafts clanked as the pistons moved in and out of cylinders with bursts of steam shooting out, and I could feel the heat from the boiler as it hissed and gurgled. As they passed I could look up at the fireman shoveling coal into a fiery maw and see the engineer in the cab, dressed in striped overalls and gloves with cuffs on them. How I envied him and wished that when I grew up I could be like him.

Often in the summer we would go up Coeur d'Alene Lake to my grandmother Thomson's summer home, Aberdeen Lodge, which was named after the city where my grandfather's parents had lived before they left Scotland. We could either drive for over twenty-five miles or take a boat there. When we went up the lake by boat my parents would sometimes take me to the wheel house, where I could watch the captain steering. I don't remember how old I was, but I remember once he let me steer and held me high enough so I could pull the rope to the whistle. At that time I wanted to be the captain on a boat. I also enjoyed watching the men in the engine room throwing big chunks of wood into the firebox and seeing all the machinery with bright and shiny brass fittings moving. I was also fascinated by the bathroom on the boat, for when I went to the toilet, it was open and the sewage dropped directly into the lake.

Some of my best early memories are of Aberdeen Lodge, a beautiful two-story log house which my grandmother Thomson had built after she obtained the property in 1910 as a homestead. She originally intended for it to be a year-around home and it was furnished appropriately. The house was surrounded by acres of property that occupied a whole bay on the lake. The property included farm land above and beside the house a stream that flowed year around. There were a number of outbuildings which included a well house, a cooler house, a barn and an outhouse. It was the scene of many parties and my parents often entertained friends, including the McCartys, the Barclays and the Edmonds, grandparents of Duane Hagadone. I remember two of our neighbors who owned adjacent property. Mr. (Eck) Ecklund was Swedish, with a very pronounced accent. (He used to call me Yorge.) Mr. Gasser lived to the east of us and had a very distinguished looking beard which was trimmed to come to a point at the chin. I remember sleeping there and being scared when the coyotes (I thought they were wolves) howled during the night. I would snuggle way down under my covers in fright. I also have a faint memory of my father shooting wood rats in the middle of the night, but I don't know if he ever hit one.

Often in the early spring we would go out to the meadows hunting for mushrooms and buttercups. There were meadows on a portion of the lake across the Spokane River on the near west side which were often flooded during high water. The moist conditions along with rich manure from cows who grazed there made it a prime area for mushrooms. I remember Dad would dress in what he considered casual clothes, a kind of olive green driving suit with a belted back and a soft colored shirt rather than his usual starched one. He might even wear a cap rather than a hat. As you might gather, he was not a man for casual attire by today's standards. We would receive a lecture on mushrooms as we hunted. Dad would look for either Meadow Mushrooms, Morels, or Shaggy Manes. The Meadow Mushrooms looked like the ones you buy in the supermarket and both the Morels and Shaggy Manes looked like they had a cone-shaped hat on. We were warned about the poisonous Amanitas and how a single bite of one would cause a horrible death. Dad would lecture on how to look for certain kinds of gills and other identifying characteristics. He also would tell about an occasion when he ate a piece of a mushroom he was not familiar with and spit it out immediately. It was half the

Aberdeen, our summer place on Lake Coeur d'Alene.

Canoeing with my cousin George Preston, in the bow.

size of the fingernail on his little finger. Even at that he became violently ill, was sick for several days and almost died. If mushrooms were served on the dinner table that night after we returned, no amount of pleading would get me to eat any. I didn't want to die!

On these outings we would also look for buttercups which often would bloom about the same time. It was quite a mysterious game. Somehow when Mother or Dad would point out places for me to hunt, I would find nickles or dimes that the fairies had left next to the buttercups. I never stopped to think about why I didn't find money by ones in other places.

A really special treat was a trip to Natatorium Park in Spokane. We would often take a picnic lunch and swimming suits and make a day of it. What a place!! There were beautifully landscaped grounds with formal flower beds, a huge indoor swimming pool, a myriad of exciting rides and a large dance pavilion where I used to dance when I was in college. Because I was a water boy, and I still am, the pool was the highlight of the day. I remember the hot moist chlorine smell as you entered the building and the excitement as I undressed and put on my suit and, wonder of all wonders, the hot water in the pool. I had reached nirvana!

Of course I enjoyed all the rides; I can't say which one the most. They had a water slide which you slid down in a boat from a tower, 100 feet high, with a pond at the bottom. That was exciting when you hit the water with a mass of spray. There was the beautiful merry-go-round, the carousel which is presently in Riverfront Park in Spokane, with all the sounds of the organ and happy cries of the children as they tried to reach out and grab the metal rings. I was scared stiff of the Jack Rabbit as we climbed to the highest points and then plummeted almost straight down and were thrown violently as we suddenly went around a tight curve. I thought I couldn't stand it, yet as soon as I got to the end I wanted to start all over again. There were the bumper cars which were my opportunity to see how well I could drive. The darned things just wouldn't go the way I steered and I was always running into other cars. I've always been afraid of heights

The Jack Rabbit at Natatorium Park. Libby photo L86-285, courtesy NWMAC/EWSHS.

Aerial photo of Natatorium Park with a portion of Fort Wright in the background. Courtesy Wallace Gamble.

and I would be petrified when I got to the top of the Ferris wheel. Of course the sandwiches we had with us were not enough; I had to have lemonade and hot dogs. I went home happy but tired!

I started to school when I was five years old. I decided I wanted to go and nothing would make me deviate. I begged and pleaded until finally my mother broke down. When the time came for me to begin and we reached the steps going up to the Central Annex, I suddenly changed my mind and my mother had to drag me up the steps kicking and screaming all the way. When I finally entered the classroom I was greeted by Miss Wahlstrom, the first grade teacher. She was beautiful and kind and had to start work on me immediately. First, she started by telling me she only had one other brown-eyed boy in the class and wanted another one. (He was Bill Glindeman who lives in Spokane and is still a friend of mine.) She was unbelievably patient with me and I adored her. Years later, when I married, we received a letter from her. She had also been my wife's first grade teacher in Spokane, two years after she taught me. In it she told various stories about the things I did in class. Apparently every time she opened a drawer in her desk I would run up to see what was in it. I guess I was enough of a headache she still remembered me twenty years later, whereas she remembered my wife as a model child.

From my very early years I was surrounded by books and fortunately I had a teacher, Bess Cruse, in the second grade, who taught me to read very well. She wasn't like my first grade teacher who was very loveable, but was tough and really made me work. She affected my whole life and I will never forget her, even though I didn't like her very well at the time. I can never remember when I was not surrounded by books. My mother began to read to me when I was very young and as soon as I could read myself I always had books. At first the *Uncle Wiggly* books, *Pinocchio*, then *Billy Whiskers* books, then the *Oz* books. These were followed by the children's classics: *King Arthur's Knights; Treasure Island; The Last of the Mohicans; Robin Hood; Robinson Crusoe, Tom Sawyer, Jibby Jones*, the *Tom Swift* series and the *Pony Rider Boys* series and others too numerous to mention. I remember some books Mrs. McCarty lent me, a series

Jules Verne had written and they sparked an interest in science fiction, which I have never lost. As I became older other books were my favorites, such as *Westward Ho*, *Two Years Before the Mast*, *The Call of the Wild*, and any and all history books. We took the *National Geographic* and archaeology became an interest of mine very early. This fascination with books has continued all my life and I still appreciate my second grade teacher.

In 1923 Dad purchased a new Studebaker which was a remarkable car. It could hold three people in the front, three in the back, and had two jump seats which folded into the floor which would hold two more people. It had two vases to hold flowers and window shades on the rear window and two side windows to provide privacy for the passengers in the back seat. It had spare tires on two sides and also had a trunk in the back with special fitted luggage designed for it. It was a great car for trips except the radiator boiled every time we went up a long hill. I remember on one trip to the coast we had to stop numerous times to cool the radiator and put in more water as we drove along the Columbia Gorge Highway.

I must have been six or seven when we moved to the big house at 817 Sherman Avenue. Dad bought it in 1924, but he built the office and did some renovation before we moved in. I loved that house! It just seemed that we had always lived there and I fitted in to my new surroundings rapidly. The house had been built in 1902 for a lumber baron, F.A. Blackwell, and was the largest in town, with grounds occupying half of a city block. It was only fitting that my father, who was probably the largest man in town, (6'5" and 225 pounds) should have a home to match. There was a porch with railings around the front and two sides and a roof supported by large cylindrical columns. The house had a huge basement with an area which could store forty cords of wood (the furnace would take four-foot sticks of wood), a wash room with tubs and a wood stove, a room for a gardener, his bathroom with tub and toilet, and a fruit and a vegetable room. In those days people canned their own fruit and many jars could be kept in the fruit room. We stored potatoes and I don't remember what else in the vegetable room.

Dad's office was attached to the main floor of the house and the entrance was off the porch on the west side. You entered the house through two front doors and a small vestibule which had a floor of red and white two-inch square tiles where people could leave their boots and rubbers. This led into an entry hall which was about twenty-five feet long, with dark stained wainscoting which ran up about four feet. The hall had a tiled fireplace at the end with beveled glass mirrors above the mantelpiece and a secret panel on the right side. I don't know what its purpose was originally, but Dad kept liquor in it during Prohibition. The hall had a twelve-foot ceiling with dark stained beams and there were huge sliding doors, ten feet high, which could close off doorways into the living room, parlor and the dining room. Each doorway had a heavy velvet portiere on each side which was held by big brass rings and slid on heavy brass poles. These could also screen the rooms. I just heard a few years ago that the portiers came originally from a house of ill repute in Butte, Montana. The living room also had paneling and a tiled fireplace with mirrors above the mantelpiece and a long bookcase with glass doors which took up most of one wall. The room on the other side, the parlor, was more informal and had no wainscoting. We called it the Green Room. It had a green carpet when we first bought the house, but we continued to call it by that name even after we changed the color of the carpet. There also was a small bathroom underneath the stairs with a marble sink and a toilet.

The dining room was outstanding. It also had the wainscoting and a large built-in buffet with lovely beveled glass mirrors in back and two sides of the center section and two cupboards on either side with doors with leaded beveled glass fronts and drawers for silverware. All the hardware for the buffet was of an ornate brass design. In the center was a beautiful satin silver light fixture, which originally cost $500, and a matching fixture on one wall. They both had frosted glass shades which were etched with a flower pattern and had almost a pastel appearance when lit. There were two narrower side windows about eight feet high and a wider center window, with a beveled leaded glass panel at the top, which would reflect a rainbow of colors throughout the room when the morning sun hit.

Ours was a gracious street, with large lots and distinguished houses. Our home is in the background to the right.

Our big house at 817 Sherman Avenue. It was originally built in 1902 by the lumber baron F.A. Blackwell. Even though my mother hired help, she worked very hard keeping this house and entertaining its many guests.

A swinging door led out of the dining room into a butler's pantry. On either side were cupboards large enough to store several twelve-piece settings of china and enough glasses for any occasion. At the end there were large bins which could hold whole sacks of sugar and flour. Off the pantry was a large kitchen where we usually ate our breakfast. It could seat the whole family including the maid, with plenty of room left over for the stove, a large work table and a double sink. There was a small closet off the kitchen for pots and pans and a back stairway to the second floor and another to the basement. A box on the wall had a bell and arrows that would point to indicate the room where a signal originated. There were push buttons in two upstairs bedrooms and a signal under the dining room table to let the maid know when the dishes were to be cleared or the next course served.

Leading from the main hall was a stairway to the second floor. The wainscoting continued up the staircase to a large landing and on to the top of the stairs. There was a balustrade which surrounded the opening at the top of the stairs and down to the hall where there was a round column which supported the bannister. I used to slide down the bannister for a number of years, until I fell one day and had the wind knocked out of me. Fortunately there were no broken bones. At the top of the stairs was another large hall with ten-foot ceilings and doors leading out of it to the bedrooms. There were three smaller bedrooms (which were still big) and one 30-foot bedroom for my parents. It originally had been two rooms, and with one wall knocked out, provided my mother with enough space for a sitting area. It was large enough for a couch, chairs and a chaise longue, which were all made of a light colored wicker. On this floor were two bathrooms, one off the master bedroom and one off the hall. Both had bathtubs and marble sinks and toilets supported by marble platforms.

Above was a third floor with two maids' rooms and one large room for parties, along with a couple of storage rooms. The large room also provided me with a place to play with my trains. It wasn't like setting up the tracks in a room downstairs; they could be left up indefinitely and I remember constructing towns out of Lincoln logs which could be assembled into log houses. We had friends who manufactured supplies for bee keepers and as they had small pieces of white pine they usually threw away, I could pick them up and put them to all sorts of creative uses. With an electric train I had been given for Christmas one year and one Bill had outgrown, I could assemble long stretches of tracks and be running two engines at one time, which often resulted in dramatic wrecks.

The move to the big house brought about changes in our life style. Sunday was more or less a family day. Bill and I would dress up in our "Sunday clothes" and go to church. Dad would often see a few patients in the office in the morning, but the rest of the day was devoted to family. Our Sunday dinners were very special with a menu of various meats carefully selected by Dad. They might be roast beef, pork, lamb, ham or even chicken and dumplings. Dad would officiate in carving and serving the meat, which he did with great aplomb and surgical skill. The knife would have to be gracefully sharpened by a few adroit strokes with the steel. Then he would delicately dissect the meat in uniform slices. The potatoes and other vegetables would be served by one of the ladies sitting to his right.

The guests could be as varied as the menu. Frequently they would be family and there were many of them at this time. My dad's brother Bramwell had moved to town with his wife Mabel and their family of two, and my mother's sister Mary had moved back from Canada after her husband's death, with her family of three. My grandmother was always included, and Mrs. McCarty and Moses Sauve would often be part of our family gatherings.

Sometimes our Sunday guests could be a colorful lot. One of them was Eugene (Gene) Reichardt, a very glamorous exiled Russian nobleman. When the Communists took over he had escaped by way of the Black Sea, but in boarding the boat in a hail of bullets, lost his right arm. He was immaculate in his dress, and his closely trimmed little mustache and his cultivated manners (with hand kissing) had the ladies all in a swoon. Getting to the more mundane, he was earning his living as an engineer for the Highway Department.

The Green Room, with Dad's chair.

Dining room sideboard decorated for Christmas. Blackwell had spared no expenses with the leaded glass and fine woodwork.

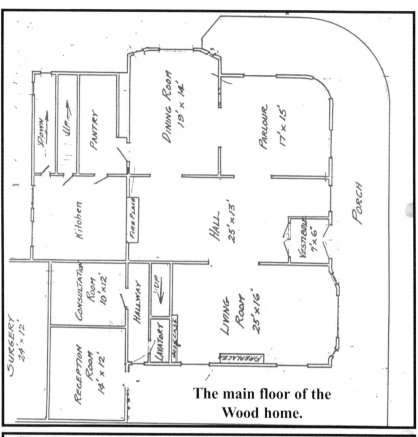

The main floor of the Wood home.

The B.R. Lewis Lumber Company, purchased by F.A. Blackwell in 1909. Inset is F.A. Blackwell. Courtesy POCHS.

Dressed in my Sunday best with older brother Bill.

We attended the Presbyterian Sunday School.

The imposing Catholic Church attended by many of my friends. My father's string quartet always performed here for Christmas Eve mass.

On Sunday nights we would have more or less an open house with buffet, which would consist of a tray of raw vegetables, cheeses, meats, breads and a dessert. Friends knew they could just stop in unannounced and that they were welcome. Often in the fall and winter, a group which included my father on the cello and Mr. Fahringer, the high school music teacher, would assemble for string quartets and quintets and they would play for hours. I remember being lulled to sleep by Brahms, Mozart and Beethoven.

Not long after we had moved to the big house my father located an old pool table somewhere and had it moved up to the third floor. Getting it there was a problem in logistics. They found they couldn't move it up the stairs so decided to hoist it up in sections through the windows, which necessitated taking them out of their casings so they could squeeze the larger parts through. Once the table was reassembled and ready for use, it provided years of pleasure for both Bill and me. Bill used to spend hours perfecting his game. It seemed he was usually able to beat everyone he played. I finally discovered the secret of his success. He had taken one of my thin pieces of white pine and placed it under one leg of the table. This changed the way the balls rolled and gave him a competitive edge, or so he thought. He probably would have won anyway. We were pretty lucky, because in those days not many kids had a pool table in their home.

In the backyard was a carriage house, dating from horse and buggy days, which had room for two cars and served as a garage. It had a hayloft above and chutes down to stalls, where they had kept the horses. When I was a little older it became my clubhouse. There was also an ice house filled with sawdust where they had originally been able to store enough ice to last them all spring, summer and fall.

One of my memories from that time was punishment. I seemed to have a penchant for getting into trouble and these errors in judgement were subject to retribution. The degree of punishment was dependent upon the severity of the offense. Usually they were minor infractions and a good switching on the legs sufficed. Boy, how that stung! To this day I can remember my brother squealing on me and then gloating as he cut the switch for my mother. Yet I can only remember one major infraction, when I set the firecrackers off underneath the car in the garage. That was followed by a spanking from my father with his razor strop. That was the only time I can remember my father spanking me. The last spanking administered by my mother was humorous. She was very small and I was too big to be spanked. When I started laughing, she joined in, and that was the end of my spankings. For failure to follow my brother's rules and regulations, the punishment consisted of his pounding me on my arms; it's a wonder my arms aren't deformed.

After the move, when I was eight, my Uncle Bill died. I hadn't spent as much time with him after I started to school and we had moved to the new house which was a couple of blocks away. I guess it was easier than it would have been a few years before, but I was still stunned. It was my first experience with the death of someone I loved.

I remember the *Georgie Oakes,* the queen of all the lake boats. She was a stern-wheeler 170 feet long with a 28-foot beam and had been built originally by the Northern Pacific in 1890 to haul passengers from their pier at Coeur d' Alene to Cataldo, where they transferred to a narrow gauge railroad to reach the Coeur d' Alene mines. On the return trip she was capable of carrying one hundred tons of ore. The boat was remodeled a number of times and changed hands once before being bought by the Red Collar Line in 1909. They ran her until 1920 when she was tied up for a number of years in the area which the Coeur d' Alene Hotel now occupies. I can remember walking by her in awe. I was angry when they took her out and burned her at a Fourth of July celebration in 1927, when I was nine years old. She broke loose from her moorings out in the lake and drifted into a boom of logs where they had to put out the fire. They couldn't even do that right; it still rankles. Think what an entrepreneur could do with her nowadays; she would be a gold mine.

As a small boy of seven or eight I was intrigued by the ritual of Dad shaving and getting dressed. He would get up and take off his night shirt (he never wore pajamas) and put on his B.V.D.s (in winter long

The *Georgie Oakes* on the St. Joe River. Courtesy MNI.

Al Lafferty's favorite tugboat, the *Cougar*. Courtesy MNI.

Lounge Area of the Georgia Oakes

A tugboat and crew pulling logs to the sawmill. Courtesy MNI.

underwear). He never wore shorts or T-shirts as men do now. Then he would shave, a process which required great care in preparation. He would wash his face followed by the application of hot steaming washcloths to soften his beard. Next came the lather. There was a cake of special shaving soap in the bottom of an ornate pink mug with a gold rim on it, along with a large brush, which he would moisten with very hot water and manipulate vigorously making up a lather. This would be brushed on, making him look like Santa Claus. He would then pick up his extremely sharp straightedged razor, open it up, give it a few swipes on his razor strop and commence shaving. Very adroitly he would proceed with long practiced strokes, stopping from time to time to wash off the soap under running water. Sometimes he might pooch out an upper or lower lip to shave that area, or use his left hand to draw down the skin to facilitate his getting a smoother shave. After he went over his face initially, he would then moisten his skin and go over his whole face with the razor again without soap. After that he would carefully assess the job he had done and if it was satisfactory wash and dry his face. Then he would splash fragrant Bay Rum on and he was ready to face his day.

After he shaved he would go into the other room and put on his shoes and socks. The socks extended up to his calf and were held up with garters clipped around the upper portion of his legs. The shoes, which were usually black, were high topped highly shined and, as I remember, either made of calf skin or kangaroo. Then he would put on his shirt. They were specially tailored and made by Belden-Evans in Minneaplis. (Just to feel elegant, I stopped in and had them take my measurements and make a shirt for me several years ago.) His shirts, with a monogram on the pocket, were white, with heavily starched cuffs which were closed with gold cuff links. The collars were detached, heavily starched and fastened to the shirt with gold collar buttons. Next came the bow tie which he also had specially made because he required such a large neck size. He would hand tie them himself, taking great care to be sure the bow was perfect. Then he would slip on his trousers, tuck in his shirt tails and pull up his suspenders; even if he wore a belt he wore them. At last the coat would go on with a white handkerchief in his breast pocket. Since my dad was such a large man, his suits, made from carefully selected wool, were all hand tailored. Having completed the ceremony he was ready for his day.

What a young boy did in those days was quite seasonal. With the advent of winter, we started planning for Christmas, which was always a very special occasion in our home and the preparations went on for weeks beforehand. Mother would make batches of cookies of various types such as gingerbread, shortbread and date-filled ones, which were my favorite. The shortbread ones were cut in the form of stars, trees, or just circles and were sprinkled with a glittery substance. The gingerbread ones were very special as much effort went into making them. They were cut out with a cookiecutter in the form of little men and women. Mother would then place a white lemon-flavored icing on them and proceed. She would mix up various vegetable dyes and, using toothpicks for a painting tool, would paint on little faces and intricate peasant costumes. When they were finished they were works of art; even as a child I didn't want to eat them because I didn't want to destroy them. Also there were fruit cakes to be made, but why I didn't know, as I didn't care for them.

There were always the Christmas scenes Mother made. I remember one which was made on a mirror using cotton for snow. There would be tiny trees, animals and little figures on sleds, sometimes little Santas; the decorations changed from year to year. They were placed on the sideboard in the dining room. Then there were the presents to be wrapped. They too were a work of art, with different colored paper layered on very scientifically and embellished with various stickers and tied with different colored strings and ribbons. I often think about how carefully they were wrapped and how callously I tore the wrappings off.

The house also was decorated with branches over the mantelpieces of the fireplaces and various colored candles all over - always a big one on the window ledge by the front door - to welcome the Christ child. My job when I was old enough was to decorate an outside tree with colored lights.

The Christmas tree was a balsam fir at least ten feet tall. It was always in the entrance hall and the scent from the fresh-cut tree would permeate the house. I remember at least one year when I went up on Tubbs Hill and cut a tree myself. After it was placed, Mother would bring out the big tin box which held all the decorations and the trimming was a meticulous ritual. First to go on would be the ornament at the top which was made of a silvered glass and started with a cylindrical shaped portion which fitted over the top of the tree. It then expanded to form a ball and tapered gracefully to a point at the top. The height of it was perhaps ten to twelve inches.

Then the lights were strung and I remember a string of Japanese lights in the shape of miniature Japanese lanterns which were delicate pastel colors, but predominantly red. Of course they were the type where if one burned out the whole string went out. This meant my first duty was to get the lights going by screwing and unscrewing bulbs until the whole string would light up. For many years the bulbs were replaceable, but the time came when if one burned out it would have to be replaced with an ugly American regular bulb. Finally, in later years, I remember Mother even tying strings around the Japanese lanterns and hanging them from the tree because they were so pretty.

After the lights were on, the next procedure was to place the icicles (tinsel) on the tree and Mother insisted they had to be placed just so. They were long narrow shiny metal strips about eighteen to twenty four inches long and were carefully draped over the branches one by one. (They were not just thrown on the tree as less tidy people were apt to do.) When they were all on they hung down to form glimmering sheets. After Christmas was over they were taken off as they had been placed, one by one, and saved for the next year.

Next, the gold and red garlands were placed on the tree and finally the ornaments. Most of them were of fragile blown glass and came from Germany. One was a lovely graceful pastel-colored swan suspended in a net of silver threads with a delicate tail which fanned out at the back. Other glass ornaments were little trumpets which could

Mother's Christmas gingerbread cookies always seemed too beautiful and realistic to eat.

Mother had her own special way of decorating the tree with ornaments that were family heirlooms.

be blown, banjoes, drums and harps, tiny birds and round balls of all different colors. Also there were little wax angels with gossamer wings and delicate little painted faces and many old odd decorations from my mother's own childhood tree. As I remember them, they were cardboard with gold tinsel circling the angel or whatever the figure was. All the effort which went into the trimming of the tree was worth it. It was gorgeous!

The string quartet Dad played in started practicing for their annual performance several weeks before Christmas. They played for the midnight mass at the Catholic Church and the group consisted of four musicians. Dad played his cello, Ray Fahringer the violin or viola, York Kildea the violin and Gordon Giles the viola. It seems to me that sometimes it may have been a quintet with Fern McFarland on the piano. It was a town ritual and the fact that most of the musicians weren't Catholic didn't make any difference.

On Christmas Eve Dad would prepare a big batch of Tom and Jerry batter which had to be carefully made. As I remember, the batter was made in the huge special china bowl in which it was served. The white of the eggs were beaten thoroughly until they were stiff and were added to the yolks which also had been beaten. Then numerous packages of powdered sugar were added along with some vanilla for seasoning and this all mixed. This process made a very thick batter. When the drinks were served, Dad used huge mugs, which were a part of the set, and first put in a couple of ounces of booze then hot water (or milk?) followed by a dollop of the batter. Dad would top this off with a dash of nutmeg and hand the mixture to a guest along with a long spoon to stir it.

I have since been told that after the quartet's arrival in the choir loft where they played, the fragrance of the Tom and Jerry drinks wafted through the air. I don't know how well they played, but the fact that the service was well attended by others who also had celebrated before their arrival probably helped.

Christmas was, I suppose one could say, a time of greed for me. Well in advance I wrote a letter to Santa or told him what I wanted. I never had to be prompted. The list was always long and well thought out. I did much snooping before Christmas after I got a little older. I remember one time I wanted a football along with some other things. In the weeks before Christmas I got into the presents in a closet where they were hidden and was discovered. When Christmas day arrived none of the presents were under my tree. My cousin, George Preston, got a football along with some of the other things I had wanted that year.

The night before Christmas was always a challenge to me. Somehow I wanted to trap Santa Claus, so one year I tied a string to my big toe and the other end to my stocking which was secured to the foot of my bed. I told my parents how clever I was and somehow when Santa arrived he merely cut the string and I didn't awaken.

I later heard from my parents about that year. They waited until I went to sleep before filling my stocking and going down stairs to put out the presents. I stayed awake most of the night and they waited and waited for the sound of my breathing to indicate I was asleep. Finally, somewhere in the wee-small-hours, Dad in exasperation said to Mother, "Why don't we just tell him?"

I was always awake at the crack of dawn, five-o'clock or earlier, when it was time to go downstairs to get our presents. I never figured it out why I got all those presents from Santa and my parents never gave me anything, but I always got plenty of loot.

I remember several special Christmas presents. One was an electric train naturally and the other was a model airplane. It was a copy of Lindbergh's *Spirit of Saint Louis* and actually flew with a propellor. When I came down that morning it was suspended from one of the ceiling beams by wires. It worked with a rheostat on a transformer like they used on electric trains. It operated a little motor connected to the propellor and it would fly in circles round and round; how high it flew depended on the setting on the rheostat. Unfortunately it intrigued my father and the other adults just as much as it did me and

I think it was worn out by the time Christmas week was over.

Next on the agenda were the preparations for dinner. They would start with the turkeys. There were two, one cooked downstairs in a big wood-range in the laundry room, the other in the electric stove in the kitchen. The birds were usually large Toms weighing twenty pounds or more. In those days it was a real chore cleaning a turkey to get it ready. There were pin-feathers to be removed and the bird had to be singed first with a piece of rolled up newspaper which would be lit with a match. Then the stuffing went in and the birds were ready to go into the oven. There were huge kettles of potatoes to be peeled along with vegetables such as peas and always rutabagas (ugh!), then bowls full of various condiments to go on the table, always Cross and Blackwell's chow chow pickles.

Dinner was a very festive occasion and we always had guests - anyone who lived alone along with other relatives - Mr. Sauve, Mrs. McCarty, Grandma Thomson, Aunt Mary and her three children along with Jim Potter (another cousin) and any other strays around town who would be lonesome. I even remember at least one year when my father's brother, my Uncle Bramwell, and his family came to dinner. It wouldn't be uncommon for there to be over twenty people at the meal. It began with a blessing, usually given by Aunt Mary, and was followed by everyone being served, which was a major undertaking.

The carving of the turkeys was a very solemn ritual presided over by my father and required preparation on his part. It was, if anything, even more elaborate than his carving at Sunday dinners. The carving knife was very carefully sharpened in the kitchen before its use. Then just before the first cuts, while standing at the head of the table, he would give the knife several nonchalant swipes on the whetting steel. This would be followed by a surgical dissection of the bird which was done with great dexterity. Everyone was allowed to express their preference and he would serve them individually. The plates would be passed on to the woman sitting at the head of the table who would add mashed potatoes, gravy and the vegetables. For that many people it took considerable time for everyone to be served and Dad scarcely had an opportunity to eat anything himself before it was time to serve seconds.

After the dinner most of the women, along with some of the youngsters, would retire to the kitchen to wash and dry the dishes. Even without a dishwasher the many hands made short work of a tedious job. All the guests would then congregate in various rooms where they would enjoy the companionship around the warm fireplace fires: children to compare presents, women engaged in their talk, and the men with their cigars, often arguing about politics, especially if my Uncle Bramwell was there.

A whimsical note: suspended in the kitchen was mother's string of wishbones from fowls who had made the supreme sacrifice for many festive occasions, all picked clean and painted with silver or gold paint.

Just hearing one of the familiar Christmas carols from those days brings back a flood of memories and I suddenly miss all the people who used to congregate around the huge table. God bless them all!

My father had an innovative mind when it came to ideas to make his children's lives more complete. I had enjoyed sleeping outside for several years, so about that time my parents had the F.O. Berg Company in Spokane make me a sleeping tent which was attached to the house with a metal frame. It was quite an affair. It had a wooden floor made of tongue-and-groove flooring which went over the porch roof and an entrance of canvas which slid open to get inside. It had a curtain on one side which could be rolled up to open it and there was room for two beds. Sometimes Bill slept in it with me, but not often. I had a little table by my bed and an old radio which my father had discarded when he got a new one. It worked well and I didn't bother with a loud speaker; I just used earphones. That way I could listen as late as I wanted and no one knew I was still awake. I woke very early and listened to the *Farmers' Home Hour* and a program called *Van and Don*, on KHQ in Spokane. My interest in radios and electric gadgets sometimes got me in trouble, which I will talk about later. The best and least conspicuous place for the tent was on the side of the house by my parents' bedroom. The windows were very big anyway and I got out to the porch by going out a window and opening a screen which swung out. I enjoyed sleeping out there so well that for quite a few years I continued to sleep there not only in the summer, but well into the fall, once until the first snowfall.

I became more aware of sounds after I moved out to my tent for a portion of the year. I began noticing the whistles at the various mills which signaled the beginning of shifts. The time depended upon distance, the Rutledge Mill first, followed by the Blackwell and the Winton mills and occasionally even the Ohio Match, if the conditions were right. Then there were the church bells, especially the Angelus from St. Thomas which rang three times a day, first at 6:00 A.M., then noon, followed by the one at 6:00 P.M. On Sundays I could hear the bell from the Presbyterian Church. During the day the boat whistles could be heard when they were about to depart for their trips up the lake and when they passed Tubbs Hill Point on their return. Then there was the whistle on the *Cougar* which had a variable pitch. It was one of a fleet of tugs owned by Al Lafferty and not infrequently, when we heard the eerie sounds from the lake in the middle of the night, the whole town knew Al was out on a toot. There were also the sounds from the whistles on the Northern Pacific locomotive and the bells from the Great Northern as it moved down the middle of Front Street just two blocks from our home.

During these years I was quite an entrepreneur. The neighbors must have hated to see me coming. I sold honey which I bought from the Thompsons, who made supplies for bee keepers, and made a slight profit on each jar I sold. It was good honey so the people got their money's worth. I also sold subscriptions to the *Open Road for Boys,* and to *Better Homes and Gardens.* I didn't have to have an allowance because I made my own pin money. If I had earned it through doing my chores as I should have, I wouldn't have gotten much anyway. While we still had a wood stove in the kitchen my chore was to keep the wood box filled. My grandmother watched one day and said I was carrying a lazy man's load. I could barely make it up the steps from the basement, as I had a load of wood in my arms that was piled higher than my head. In the summer I was supposed to do watering and there was a tremendous area of lawn. It wasn't so bad with the rest of the yard where I could set sprinklers, but the parking strip had to be watered by hand and I soon got bored with that. Ralph Rosenberry, across the street, had to water his parking strip also, so we were standing there one day and started a water fight. Soon we were out in the middle of the street with our hoses trying to drench each other and stopping traffic. It was not only the main street in the city, but it was also a stretch of transcontinental highway. You can bet we both heard about that. Bill did the mowing then. After I got a little older and Bill was on to other things, I had to do it.

The McMannimans lived next door and had a son, Eddie, who became my best friend even though he was a year or two older than I. His parents were wonderful people and one of the highlights of my life, when I was ten years old, was several weeks one summer spent at their cabin by a logging camp on the Little North Fork of the Coeur d'Alene River. Eddie's father Bronc ran all the logging camps in that area for the Winton Lumber Company. The camps were spread over a wide area in the mountains and, since there were no roads for motor cars, we had to ride horseback in order to visit them. That was a real treat for me as I had never ridden a horse before. We visited at least five different camps.

Logging was very labor intensive in those days. It was before the days of chain saws and the trees were usually felled by men using two-handed bucksaws and axes. After the tree was down they would use axes to cut off the limbs and a man with a team of horses would drag the trees, either to be stacked along the river or to a location where they could be moved by some other means.

One day we rode to a camp along a narrow trail which was at least a couple hundred feet above the river. I remember I was so scared I wanted to get off and walk. They told me I was safer on the horse, but I was still scared because it didn't seem to me the trail was wide enough for a horse. Another time we rode up to a camp where they cut logs which were floated down to the river in a flume (a large trough) which was 21 miles long. Because there was a tremendous drop in elevation the logs moved at a high rate of speed at times and I was told some of the lumberjacks would ride the logs down when they were in a hurry to go home on a weekend. Needless to say it was very dangerous as the logs sometimes were thrown out of the flume.

They had many methods of getting the logs down to the river besides the flume. In places they would slide them down steep slides directly into the river. In one case they had a donkey engine (an engine powered by steam) which was down in a valley and had a cable attached to it almost a mile long which ran up the long hill to a slide made out of logs called a chute. They would attach the steel cable to logs and pull them down on the chute, which they lubricated with grease. I remember one of these "grease monkeys" was a young man only a few years older than I.   A lot of logs were moved with powerful teams of horses; they had several hundred horses in the camps in this one area.

The longest ride I made was when we rode fifteen miles down the river to the site of a log dam which they were building, supposed to be the longest log dam in the world. The horse I rode that day was used to a heavier and more experienced rider and tried to buck me off several times, once in the middle of the river which we were fording. They told me to yank up on the reins and not let him get his head down, which I did. It worked!

In the summer months they moved the logs stockpiled along the banks down the river by a series of log dams. They would allow the water to back up behind the dams for a couple of days and then flood the logs down from one dam to the next. It was exciting to watch, as the river rats (the loggers who worked on the river) would ride the logs down the river standing up.

At times the logs would be held up by some obstruction causing a log jam, which might be as high as a house. To break it up, someone had to go out and determine which was the key log and remove it. I remember watching Eddie's father going out with the logs towering over him to move one log with a peevee to break up the jam. It was horribly dangerous because the jam could have broken up at any moment and crushed him. If he was unsuccessful at that they had to use dynamite, but not if they could help it as that destroyed valuable timber.

The loggers would continue to move the logs farther and farther down until they reached the mouth of the Coeur d'Alene River at Harrison, where they would be sorted out at what they called a sorting gap. As the logs had been stamped at each end prior to being dumped into the river, the companies would identify their logs and put them into long booms to be towed down Coeur d' Alene Lake to the mills for sawing.

These logging techniques had been in use for many years, but in less than ten years, with the advent of trucks and other mechanical devices, they became outmoded. The lumberjacks themselves were a special breed of men. Ethnically they were a mixed group. There were French Canadians (some from Maine), Swedes and Norwegians from Minnesota and Irish from all over. There was a preponderance of bachelors, as many of them stayed at camp winter and summer and just went to town occasionally for recuperation. Even their clothing was distinctive. They wore long underwear winter and summer, plaid lumberjack shirts, levis which were stagged (cut off high and allowed to unravel with threads hanging down) and held up with black suspenders and a hat with no crease in the crown. They always wore good wool socks and their boots were very special, usually handmade with hobnails or caulks on the soles.   The type of boot depended upon what type of work the men did. The caulks (corks) were screwed into the soles of the boots worn by river rats, who needed the sharp points to hold them on the slippery logs in the river. Usually the other loggers wore hobnailed boots.

As they couldn't smoke in the woods a large number of the loggers chewed tobacco in various forms. With the Scandinavians it was "snoose," (Copenhagen) which came in round tins. They would pack it in the space between there lower lip and their front teeth and would go around looking like they had a swollen lip. Others chewed "Star" cut plug which came in small bars, from which they would cut small pieces with their pocket knives to be chewed. It was flavored with licorice and was probably the tastiest. Many of them chewed "Beech-nut" which was shredded and came in a packet; this would be held between their upper back teeth and their cheek.

There were other special men around the camps in those days. Since there were no roads for trucks to haul supplies to the other camps most of the hauling was done with pack strings. It was a real art to load a string of mules properly. They used a special type of saddle and since there was a vast variety of articles to be carried, it was difficult to tie them on with ropes so they wouldn't slide off with the movements on the trail. They were tied on with what was called a "diamond hitch." The men who handled the animals (not always mules) were called mule skinners, and they were noted for their profanity! I had an opportunity to find out one day. They loaded the supplies destined for other camps at Honeysuckle where we were staying. The mule skinner had just finished packing a whole string of mules with supplies and one of the mules started to buck. Before it was over the whole string was bucking and kicking and nothing the man could do would stop them. They bucked until kegs of nails had fallen to the ground and the tops of the kegs kicked in, and sacks of flour and sugar were spilled all over the ground and cans of food of various types were spread all over. The mule skinner didn't stop swearing once, it was continuous and I don't think he repeated the same words twice!

I suppose another thing that interested a small boy was the food. For breakfast the loggers ate prodigious amounts. They would eat plate-sized flapjacks stacked four or five inches high, along with sausages, ham or bacon, eggs, fried potatoes, jam, jelly and toast. All of this was washed down with gallons of coffee. There was a sideboard where they had the makings for sandwiches which they took with them, as they worked through their lunch hour.

Dinner consisted of at least two kinds of roast meat, mashed potatoes,

Greasing the log flume. MNI.

Skidding with horses. MNI.

With my friend Eddie, left.

A logging camp meal. MNI.

Floating logs down the Coeur d'Alene River. Courtesy MNI.

Eddie and I en route to another logging camp.

gravy, several kinds of vegetables, condiments and plates of bread stacked high. You had to be careful when you reached for a slice of bread because you might get stabbed with a fork, as the loggers would just spear it with their forks. Then for dessert they would have at least a couple of kinds of pie and cake, doughnuts and cookies. The food was all excellent because the loggers worked terribly hard and burned up lots of calories and demanded good food. If it wasn't good they would raise hell!

That winter was a good one for skating and when Eddie got new tube skates I had to have a pair. I'll never forget the day I got my new skates. Eddie had already left for the lake by the time I got home. After I arrived at Fernan I looked all around to show him my new prized possessions, but didn't find him. When I got home that evening my mother told me my father was over seeing Eddie and that he was very sick. When he got home about an hour later he told me Eddie had died. He had spinal meningitis and had died in just a couple of hours after the onset of the disease. I couldn't believe he was dead and going to his funeral was my first crushing personal defeat. I had been praying for a couple of days and I felt if I prayed hard enough he would come back to life.

After that it was different when I went next door. Eddie's parents were very good to me and it seemed his mother couldn't do enough for me. She made wonderful chocolate cake and I remember her feeding it to me frequently. They had two Shetland ponies which I wanted to ride, but they bucked a lot and I was afraid to get on them, even though they liked me because I fed them apples. I have a picture of me on one of them so I must have ridden him at least once. But I missed Eddie terribly.

The next summer I would walk down by the docks which were already becoming splintered and dilapidated because of disuse. They covered a large area and just a portion of them were still being used. There were a number of boats which were no longer in use tied to pilings out in the lake, a carry-over from the time when there had been over fifty steamboats operating on the lake. I started taking our boat out almost every day, because I was still lonely. The canoe was called a St. Lawrence double-ender because it had oarlocks and could either be rowed or paddled. Mr. Sauve, who had come out from Canada because of my grandfather and was related to my grandmother, built boats for sale and rental. He kept an eye on me and taught me how to handle a boat under all kinds of conditions while I was still very young. I would often pretend I was a French fur trader or an Indian and quietly paddle around all the rocks and inlets on the other side of Tubbs Hill and sometimes even across the lake. Apparently my mother never worried when I was on the lake because I could swim and was cautious.

Down by Sauve's there were still boats operating out of the Red Collar line docks. The *Flyer*, at 130 feet long, was the largest of the boats still in use, while the *Radio* and *Clipper* were smaller. The *Rambler*, a small tug, was also docked there. The *Miss Spokane*, a beautiful big boat 140 feet long,which ran for less than one year, was also tied to the their docks for many years. I enjoyed watching them load the boats with passengers, wagons, plows, sacks of sugar, and flour, which they hauled to farms around the lake.

The summer of 1929, when I was eleven, my old friend Dick Fischer and I made a trip up the lake which lasted for several days. We camped on the beaches and built fires and cooked our own food. I remember we went to bed when it got dark and got up when the sun came up in the morning. We slept in sleeping bags and tried cutting some balsam branches to cushion us from the ground. It may have been what the fur traders did, but it didn't work for us; the ground was still hard. I was too young to go to Boy Scout camp yet, but I remember we stopped at the camp one morning when they were just getting up. We had already cooked our breakfast and traveled for some distance. We felt sorry for them because they were so regimented and we were free as a breeze. I felt the same the next year when I was twelve and went to camp myself. I got an award for being a good camper, but I missed the freedom to do what I wanted when I wanted.

Later that same summer the family went on a vacation which was

Steamboat docks at Coeur d'Alene with busses picking up passengers bound for Colville and Spokane. Courtesy MNI.

Red Collar Line boats in winter at Lake Coeur d'Alene. Courtesy MNI.

The steamboat docks at the city of Coeur d'Alene became a hub of activity from the town's inception. During my early years, boats were still a part of our lives. When we went downtown we could see the boats, hear their whistles as they were coming and going day and night, and we often traveled on them. The Red Collar Line was in stronger condition financially than it had been, but with the advent of automotive transportation, business continued to deteriorate. Boat after boat was retired until the only passenger boats still running were the *Rambler*, *Radio*, *Clipper* and *Flyer*. To add insult to injury, Hawley's Auto Interurban Bus Company imported the *Comet* from Lake Chelan in 1926, providing new competition. In retaliation, the Red Collar formed a bus company with each bus topped with a Red Collar Stack.

When Herrick's empire collapsed in 1929, the Red Collar Line Company was again forced into bankruptcy. Potlatch Forests then purchased the company, but business continued to decline. Daily schedules were first reduced to two or three times weekly, then to once a week or Sundays only. Finally the one large steamboat remaining, the *Flyer*, was used for Sunday excursions only. About 1938 all passenger and freight service were discontinued.

This left one boat, the *Seeweewanna* (Hawley's *Comet*), in passenger business. John Finney took it over in 1932, leased it for two years and purchased it in 1934. John continued to operate the *Seeweewanna*, usually coupled to the *Dancewana*. He operated them along with some smaller boats over a period of about 50 years.

different. In past vacations we had stayed at hotels along the way, but that year Dad decided we would stay in tourist cabins, which were new in our area. They were not like modern motels, as you had to take your own cooking utensils, tableware and bedding. By our present standards they were rather primitive. Instead of windows they had shutters, which could be raised and lowered, and screens. They would have a sink and cook stove (sometimes wood) and beds and some-times bathing facilities or inside plumbing.

The dock at Coeur d'Alene with Tubbs Hill in the background.

A log rolling contest beside the tugboat *Cougar*. Both MNI

My parents must have taken some time to plan for this vacation as they had paid a great deal of attention to detail. Dad had obtained for the 1923 Studebaker what he called a boot, which was a canvas-covered top like a box which fitted over another box and was secured with a strap around it. In it he placed all the kitchen needs, enameled dishes and cups, silverware, salt and pepper shakers, seasonings, spatulas, carving knife and fork, big spoons and dishrags and dishtowels. He had separate canvas bags made for iron frying pans and lids and for a coffee pot. He was ready for whatever came up. There were also two long duffel bags with drawstrings to carry the bedding.

Dad always believed in leaving at the "crack of dawn." In this case it was before dawn had cracked! It was still dark when we started and after we got a short distance from Spokane, Dad had to stop and have a nap. The roads were rather primitive in those days; the one to Spokane was paved, but from there on they were graveled, if we were lucky. After we left Pasco, the road took off across the desert with planks to cross the sand. Woe be unto you if you strayed, for you would be stuck in the sand! By nightfall we did make it to Arlington, where we stayed in the Arlington Hotel. To me it was the height of luxury, with wash basins in our rooms.

The next morning we were up early and on our way to Portland. What a day driving along the old Columbia River Highway. It was a miracle with the road often virtually hanging to the sides of cliffs with tunnels, stonework bridges and walls and beautiful vistas, all this amidst lush green growth almost like a tropical rain forest because of all the moisture. There were many thin falls hanging from the sides of the cliff above, including Multnomah Falls which is world famous. It was hectic for us, though. Every time there was much of an ascent, the radiator would boil and we would stop at little springs alongside the road to fill it up.

The first night we stayed in a cabin midway along the Columbia River Highway in Oregon. It was in an area up and away from the river as I remember it, heavily forested with firs and fragrant cedar trees. Later I remember staying in various cabins along the coast starting at

Newport where we went deep-sea fishing. That was a sad event for my father, as the seas were so rough ours was the only boat which crossed the bar that day. Dad got violently seasick which was not unexpected considering the fact that he could get seasick in a swing. He was lying on a bench at the stern of the boat and they pulled fish in right over him. All he wanted to do was die. I didn't get sick but did feel a little peaked.

I remember stopping at places along the coast we still visit frequently, such as Cannon Beach and Hay Stack Rock. We took the car down on the beach and I remember being scared we would get stuck in the sand, as we saw some people who did. We also stopped at Seaside and went swimming in a large indoor heated saltwater pool. It was always an event when I had an opportunity to swim in any pool.

I don't think anyone enjoyed out-of-town vacations with his family any more than my father. He was a different person when he escaped from the telephone and the doorbell. He would laugh and joke and sing and tell us about the various geographic oddities we were passing. I remember his singing "I've been working on the railroad" and all of us joining in on the "Dinah don't you blow" refrain. That trip still ranks as one of the happiest experiences of my life.

A typical tourist court of the period. Libby photo L87-1.42472-30, NWMAC/EWSHS.

The scenic Columbia River Highway, on the route of my most
memorable vacation. Postcard L93-42.200, courtesy NWMAC/
EWSHS.

Mother, Dad and I beside our 1929 Buick rigged for camping.

That was one of the few times I had an opportunity to go on an extended vacation with my father. The home life of a physician's family in those days pretty much revolved around his practice. We often went for rides on Sundays with Dad and sometimes he would even stop to make a call, otherwise we didn't get to see very much of him except at meal time. Even our meals were frequently interrupted by phone calls. We ate in the kitchen for breakfast and lunch and the maid would sit with us for these meals. Dad loved to cook and had some specialties. One was his onions and fried potatoes. Another was when he cooked "bloaters," which were dried, salted, smoked herrings, packed in wooden boxes from Nova Scotia. He would first soak them in water, then place them in a wire rack and take them down to the furnace and broil them over the wood coals. They smelled horrible, but tasted surprisingly good.

As a young boy I looked forward to trips to Spokane and meals at the Davenport Hotel. No matter how many times I walked into the hotel I was overwhelmed by the potpourri of sound, smells and sights; the huge ornate lobby, the massive carved wooden furniture, the scent of flowers and the splash of water in a central fountain swarming with goldfish, the singing of birds in cages, the crackling and the smell of the wood fire in the fireplace at one end and the high childish voice of the miniature bellboy paging people. Leaving the lobby I would walk past a flower shop banked with masses of fragrant flowers, past the wood-paneled coffee shop with dark eighteenth-century paint-ings of fish, vegetables, and dead waterfowl hanging on the walls. On the entrance to the dining room on the right was a wall formed by a glass tank with goldfish swimming in it. Finally, walking into the Italian Gardens, at the corner of one end was a mass of flowers, a splashing fountain and two glass cylinders on either side containing swimming goldfish. There were waitresses attired in Italian peasant costumes circling tables covered with starched white linen tablecloths, with folded napkins, heavy silver-plated monogrammed tableware, and a cleverly folded napkin containing crackers.

The climax came when I was allowed to order for myself. Although their menu was extensive, mine wasn't. It didn't vary and it was a la carte. I don't know why my parents allowed it, because it must have been expensive and it would suffice for several days' meals for me now. I always ordered crab cocktail with thousand island dressing, chicken gumbo soup, rare roast beef au jus, mashed potatoes, peas, hard rolls, and French vanilla ice cream.

The menu might sound mundane now, but at the Davenport in those days it was not. Their dressings didn't come out of gallon jars made commercially and their thousand island dressing was no exception. It was a recipe of Chef Edward Mathieu, which somehow my mother wheedled out of him. He was a world-class chef and everything that came out of his kitchen was superb. The crab cocktail, served in a small silver cup which was fitted into a larger silver cup, was surrounded by a bed of chipped ice. The chef was noted for his chicken gumbo soup and also the oval-shaped oyster crackers which came with it. The plate with the main course arrived with a silver cover over it, which was removed with a flourish when the dish was served. Naturally, the roast beef was rare and succulent. The mashed potatoes were not lumpy and cold and the peas were fresh anytime of the year. Last but not least, the French vanilla ice cream came in a chilled silver goblet and was rich and creamy. When my father paid the check, the silver change would all be bright and shiny, as they washed and polished their silver coins every night. Sometimes my father would let me keep one of the silver dollars.

Entrance to the Davenport Hotel from the Sprague Avenue.
Courtesy NWMAC/EWSHS.

**The main dining room of Davenport's Restaurant in 1919.
Courtesy Walt and Karen Worthy.**

Davenport's Restaurant and Hotel. Courtesy NWMAC/EWSHS.

A Davenport waitress. Courtesy Walt and Karen Worthy.

My memories of the Thirties were pleasant, but for many they were tough; it was during the Depression and some people had to do without a lot. However, we were not separated by the bitterness and anger which existed in many areas. In Coeur d'Alene, in our pre-high school years, we were separated more by whether we went to the Catholic or the public school and also by what public school we attended. We kind of had our neighborhood gangs and there was no discrimination because of social or economic levels.

The neighborhood gangs of course were broken up into boys and girls and there was certainly no thought in those years of such sissy

Prince, a dog any boy could love.

activities as dancing and dating girls. They were not gangs as we think of them of now, but were really a group of boys living in one section of town. We did condescend to the girls joining us in an evening game of kick-the-can if there weren't enough boys to make the game interesting, but usually we went our own ways.

Besides, a good dog was more important than any girl. My favorite dog was named Prince, in fact all my dogs were named Prince. They didn't last too long because we lived on Sherman and the traffic took its toll. But my special Prince was a big ugly, smelly Airedale about as big as I was. He had matted wiry hair that was dark on his back and sides and tan elsewhere. His coat was oily and smelly naturally, but particularly odoriferous when it was wet. He was truly a dog any boy could love. He wouldn't have made much of a watchdog as he was too friendly, but he could go wherever I did, except to school. He would follow me on my bike or all over Tubbs Hill when I was exploring with my friends. Alas, one Sunday morning, when I was at Sunday School, he met his demise, thanks to a careless motorist. My heart was broken.

I can't say what the girls did, but it was a rich life for the boys. We could even while away hours on such a simple game as mumblety-peg (mumble-the-peg), every boy had his jackknife, which was all anyone had to have to play the game. It consisted of a series of maneuvers throwing our knives in such a way the point would stick in the ground. The flips got more complicated as the game progressed, starting with flipping the knife with the thumb and forefinger, to the next finger and down to the little finger, gradually progressing from knees to wrists and elbows to shoulders and then from one ear then the other, etc. The loser was forced to extricate, with his teeth, a match stick driven into the ground.

What we did depended on the seasons. In winter we had snowball fights which often became rowdy neighborhood fracases. We also had our sleds and our skates. We could slide on many hills around town, but the most exciting one started at the reservoir on Tubbs Hill and descended precipitously down the hill around boulders and trees, often with mangled bodies littering the course.

In my younger years I had skates which clamped on my shoes, but I really was excited when I received my first pair of "tube" skates which were, of course, mounted on shoes. We also had our choice of many places to skate. Sometimes we flooded the Rosenberry's tennis court where we had noisy and aggressive games of hockey, punctuated with much profanity. In some years the ice was particularly good at Fernan, which became the center for games of crack-the-whip. A line of us would skate hand in hand and the boy at one end would suddenly come to a dead stop and the rest of us would whip and catapult the boy at the other end across the ice at breakneck speed.

Not every year, but when the winters were especially cold, we could skate on Coeur d'Alene Lake. If it was really cold we could skate out past Tubbs Point to the main channel of the lake. Frequently the ice wasn't as thick there as closer to shore and we could hear a booming sound as we skated across it. It then became a matter of derring-do to see how long we persisted when we could even see cracks forming. Providentially, none of us ever fell through the ice.

In the spring we could hardly wait to get out and roam over Tubbs Hill, sometimes even bringing home wild flowers for our mothers. Or we would play soldiers and Indians covering a good deal of the hill with our games. We of course had to be searched for wood ticks when we got home and if one burrowed in, it would have to be extricated with various bizarre rituals, such as applying the lighted end of a cigarette to it or anointing it with turpentine.

We also played marbles in the spring. There were different kinds of marbles: steelies which were steel ball bearings; aggies which were the most prized and were made out of agate; glassies, which were glass; and migs, which were baked clay and were the most commonplace. Marbles were placed in a circle drawn in the dirt, the object of the game being to knock the other guys' marbles out with your shooter. Often, but not always, the steelies were used as shooters. To do this it was necessary to hold your knuckles down on the dirt and shoot with another marble held between your thumb and forefinger, flipping it with your thumb. If you were very good and liked to gamble, the game was played for keeps. If not, you either just played with migs or not at all. You wouldn't risk losing aggies.

Maybe a little later I indulged in an activity with Dick Fischer that would surely have gotten us into trouble if either one of our parents had known. Dick's parents had two grocery stores for a time, one of them at Rathdrum, which was more farm oriented, where they sold dynamite. Apparently Dick had watched an uncle using it, so he knew more than I did about how to use it. Anyhow he stole a number of sticks from the store along with caps and some waterproof fuse. We went out in the canoe to the center of the lake and tied several sticks of dynamite together, along with some weights, inserted a length of fuse into a cap, then slit one stick and inserted the cap into it. (I cringe when I think of how we must have crimped the cap - with our teeth?) Next we lit the fuse, threw it in the lake and rowed like hell! What a tremendous explosion!! Better than the Fourth of July! A big bulge of water would rise to the surface along with debris from the bottom. (But no fish, because there wasn't very good fishing in Coeur d' Alene at that time.) I was lucky to grow up.

I did seem to do more unacceptable things with Dick than anyone else. My father had rather strong negative feelings where it came to guns, not even allowing me to have a BB gun. He had taken care of too many youngsters who lost the sight in an eye with them, or had been killed or maimed in accidents by guns, even so-called empty guns. I would go out quite often with Dick squirrel shooting, unbeknownst to my parents. We even took out his .22 in the boat once and shot at bottles floating in the lake. Because of my transgressions, I got to be quite a good shot.

We could go down to Sander's Beach to swim, or around Tubbs Hill skinny dipping. When it was the latter, we went around to the three-story cave where we swam. We were a motley crew, some of us tall, some short, dressed in various types of nondescript clothes, as boys were not out to impress anyone in those days. There were about eight or ten of us in the gang and some of us rode our bikes and the rest walked. During the summer months it didn't seem to make any difference whether our friends went to the Catholic school or the Central Annex. However, as soon as the summer was over and school began in the fall, we used to say all kinds of scurrilous things as we passed the brick wall where the "Cat-likkers" hung out, many of them friends from the summer before. We didn't call out too loudly though, as they were pretty tough kids.

We didn't have television, but there were other sources of entertainment for growing boys. A good fire was something all normal boys delighted in and we had a number of scorchers. The fire at the Coeur d' Alene Mill was outstanding; we had to stand a block away and I can remember even from that distance the heat from the flames on my face. First the mill proper caught fire, then the stacks of lumber, at least fifteen feet high, which were drying and were spread out over acres of land. (They air dried lumber in those days, not in a kiln.)

The fire at Brautigam's boat works was another hot one. I remember the old sternwheeler, the *Harrison*, burned in that one. It was in the middle of the night and I don't know how all of us knew there was a big fire - I guess it was just the sixth sense all boys possessed when it came to fires in those days. There was also the fire by the old city dock which burned Pete Johnson's old boat works where some of the big boats, such as the *Miss Spokane* were built. Of course there was the old Central School fire. It was an old large building with a bell tower, which my mother had attended. It seems to me that fire occurred during Christmas vacation and sparked the usual festivities a bit.

The Fourth was our most important occasion in the summer. We saved for months to buy firecrackers, Roman candles, rockets and anything else which would make a bang or light up the night skies. Thousands of people came to town even in those years. The Great Northern had special excursion trains and many more came in their own cars. The Red Collar Line had special trips up the lake which would return in time in the evening for people to enjoy the fireworks. There was a parade in the morning with the National Guard and all their guns and equipment and various floats. In the afternoon they had boat races, various swimming and diving competitions, a band concert and pretty girls from out of town to look at. At night after dark they would have the firework display. They shot the fireworks off from a barge out in the lake in front of the park. Every few years, if the pyrotechnists were not careful, a stray spark would set off all the displays at once and the men would end up diving into the lake while the rockets were going all different directions. That shortened the evening, but made it more exciting.

I did have a memorable experience one Fourth. I was carrying a package of fire crackers in my back pocket and was using a punk, a stick of wood with a slow-burning material glued on, to light my firecrackers. Inadvertently I somehow put it into my back pocket lit, which set the firecrackers off. It was worse than having one's pants on fire. I was madly jumping around hitting my pocket, howling and screaming for someone to help me as they were going off and what could they do? They didn't know what to do except laugh at my plight. If we had been around the lake they could have thrown me in I guess. In any case it wasn't as bad as could have been anticipated, as I don't remember even being burned.

In the fall I went into mourning, because I hated to have summer end. I continued to go out in my boat all by myself even when no one else was boating. I especially remember the fall when we launched an eight-foot punt which my father and I had built. We had worked months building it and it was our masterpiece. I think it was really the most difficult piece of carpentry my father ever attempted. I enjoyed the new boat so much I continued to row around in it almost until the first snow fell.

I guess the one redeeming thing about fall may have been Halloween. We looked forward to it for months ahead, planning deviltry we were going to accomplish. We didn't trick or treat; I guess you could say we just tricked. When we soaped windows we used wax. There were still a few outhouses around and we mapped out all the ones which were readily available. We tipped them over and always searched for one that was occupied to overturn. Our plan was to knock it over door side down.

One year we plotted for months on a supreme move. We had an old lumber cart available and an outhouse in a convenient location. We loaded the outhouse onto the lumber cart and proceeded down alleys from Eleventh and Front on our way to the city's main intersection at Fourth and Sherman, where we were going to set it up. Sadly, we got caught by the police about a block from our destination and were forced to return it to its rightful location.

The Saturday matinees at the Dream or Liberty theaters provided another form of entertainment for young boys. We weren't allowed to go to movies at night nor on Sundays, so that was our time. I would make an afternoon out of it, usually starting with a hamburger and a glass of milk at Harley Hudson's, followed by the movie. They were practically always cowboy movies and we each had our own heroes;

mine were Tom Mix and Hoot Gibson. They might kiss their horse, but never the girl, and after doing their good deeds would ride off into the sunset. We might consider an occasional Tarzan movie, but not often.

I was also interested in anything electrical. I had been given a game with an electric buzzer and I soon figured out a way to run a long wire with it and use it for a warning device. I first set it up in the cupola of the barn which we reached with a ladder. From there I could warn Leonard Gottschalk, my good friend who lived across the street, of the enemy's approach, when he was downstairs on the first floor. I don't remember now who the enemy might have been, probably girls. I next had some idea of running the wire from the third floor of the house to the basement. I don't know how I figured it, but I drilled a hole from the third floor down and somehow came out in the ceiling over the landing going up from the main floor. Mother wasn't too happy about that, even though it really was a very small hole. That ended the endeavor, however.

I had been given a set of power tools several years before, which included a lathe, circular saw and jigsaw. Although I hadn't come up with any remunerative uses for the other equipment I stumbled on a use for the jigsaw almost by accident. That year, jigsaw puzzles were the fad and I was given one and enjoyed putting it together. I thought of making one of my own, using a thin piece of plywood to paste a picture on and then cutting out a puzzle. The problem was the wood was too thick, so I experimented with various types of cardboard, which were better but not good enough. Then my father suggested a heavy dense cardboard that was used with x-rays in the hospital, where they had an unlimited supply. That was perfect! I would glue a picture to this material and cut out the puzzles and sand off any rough edges and voila! I had produced a beautiful puzzle! One night Mr. Wilson, who owned a drugstore, was at our home for dinner and my dad showed him the puzzles I had made. He was very impressed and asked me if I would like to make some and let him sell them in his store. I agreed and went to Spokane with my mother where I found some prints at John W. Grahams, which were more interesting than ordinary puzzles, and went into production. Somewhere I found a source for boxes to put the puzzles in and I delivered a few to Wilson's Pharmacy. They sold like hot cakes; apparently the people liked mine better than the commercial ones. The drugstore would buy all I could produce and I had enough spending money to satisfy all my needs. Whenever I needed a few bucks I would make a few jigsaw puzzles.

I did need money for the soda fountain at Wilson's Pharmacy. I became a chocaholic at an early age and I had to have hot fudge sundaes or chocolate milkshakes or malted milks to keep going. The milkshakes and malts in those days were made in a metal mixer that would hold about two big glasses, and they were so thick you couldn't drink them with a straw. At my age now I shudder to think of the amount of cholesterol they must have contained, but I don't think that was a danger with a growing boy.

It seems Dad always had to have his projects, I guess to take his mind off some of the sorrow which came with his profession. There was the one year my mother wanted a rock garden and Dad wanted a birdbath. He commenced on a combination rock garden and birdbath and I seem to remember he used an old hot water tank for kind of a framework for it. He worked on it for some weeks and even piped water into it, so water ran down the face of it into the birdbath. With a step in front it resembled a Catholic shrine, which some of the Catholic women who worked for us seized upon. On their way out to the clothes reel they had to pass the birdbath and if my dad happened to be looking out the office window, they would kneel and genuflect. Later, one of the priests from the church was in Dad's office seeing him and Dad asked if there wasn't something which could be done about some of the members of his flock who were doing such acts of piety and not getting any credit for it. The father responded, "Yes there is," and said, "I'll be down tomorrow morning." The next morning he came with one of the brothers from the church and hung a medal on the birdbath and blessed it. Henceforth my father insisted until he died that he had the only Catholic shrine in a Masonic backyard in America.

Dad's "shrine," the only Catholic shrine in a Masonic backyard.

The next project was his barbecue, which was really innovative. No one else in Coeur d'Alene up to that time had ever even thought of something like it. It was in two parts, a charcoal grill with an electric spit, which could be attached to it, and a stove portion with a firebox which could take two-foot lengths of wood. The stove portion also had a Dutch oven for baking. It was all made with brick and mortar. The castings for the firebox and the grill were made by the Union Ironworks in Spokane and the sheet metal work for the hood of the grill and the oven was done by Archie Holt, whom my dad called his artistic blacksmith. The stove tops, which were one half inch thick, were made from the old Coeur d'Alene Mill burner doors. Dad picked them up somewhere after the mill burned. The stove portion had a firebox which took two-foot lengths of wood, and the smoke and heat passed over an oven built into the stove, then down the side, underneath it and then in back of it up to the stack. The charcoal grill and barbecue was to one side as a separate entity. It was waist high, built of brick and covered with a steel cap on the top, with hinged doors that opened in front. The grill, which was used to grill steaks, lamb chops, etc., was removable, so it wouldn't be in the way when

Dad in chef's apron and cap.

the barbecue was in use.   The meat was placed on a spit that extended out the back side and rested on a metal notched strip on the right.   Someone invented an ingenious series of wheels to gear down the speed of the spit, and a belt ran from the electric motor to the wheels and another to the spit.   Without knowing it, my dad had succeeded in designing the "French Range."

I don't think my dad even dreamed the barbecue would be so successful.   He loved to cook for whole gangs of people, up to twenty or thirty.   There were restaurant-sized pots and pans which he used and everything could be done out there.   He would buy a big prime rib roast of beef, sometimes as long as 18 inches, and have the butcher roll it, so it could be cooked on the spit.   In the summer we would have creamed new potatoes with mint, ears of fresh corn and maybe baked beans, which were cooked in the oven, and the barbecued beef.   Of course Dad would take credit for cooking the food, but Mother would work for hours before and afterwards when we had these dinners for so many guests. Although he had limited time, Dad also helped me with several projects which I never could have done on my own. Fortunately, our big house had a large basement workshop area equipped with a sturdy work bench and vises. There was also a work area in the upstairs of the barn-garage. At an early age I had been given a set of Stanley tools; saw, plane, chisels, hammer, brace and bits and coping saw.

My first serious project with Dad was a boat, an eight-foot punt rowed with oars. In addition to my dad's help, the advice of Moses Sauve from the boat works proved essential for this project. In fact, Mr. Sauve made a beautiful pair of spoon oars for me. Dad would work with me in the early mornings and evenings. The launching at Suave's boat works, although it did not include champagne, was impressive. We had a bottle of some kind which we broke over the prow as the boat slid into the water.

Another memorable project with my dad was no less than a castle. In school I loved history and had a fine high school teacher for ancient history. For a class project, I decided to make a castle and learned all I could about them. The whole castle was built of white pine and started out with just boards. The walls were made of strips of wood cut out on my circular saw and these strips were sawed with notches to give the pieces the appearance of individual stones. The strips were then placed on top of one another so they looked like a wall built of stone. The castle had turrets, notched walls, a keep, a draw-bridge and a portcullis. The completed castle was painted gray and the roofs red to resemble tile. For the moat, my mother helped by mixing up gelatin, which gave it the appearance of water. Again, Dad had entered into the building with me, although I did most of the actual work. I got an A for the project, but the greatest benefits were studying about castles, actually building the castle, and working with my father.

My mother also had her projects, the most absorbing of which was her garden, but my energetic father also shared in this effort. Both of my parents spent many winter evenings perusing various catalogs,

Mother and I launch the punt at Sauve's boatworks. Moses Sauve was a superb French Canadian boat builder.

The maiden voyage of the punt.

including Burpee's Annual. Then months ahead of time, they would order the seeds for the next summer. They would decide where the various plants would go and make a chart of the whole garden. My dad made a cold frame in which they would start the seeds ahead of time before setting the young plants out in the spring. Mother grew a profusion of both vegetables and flowers, and her garden became a showplace in Coeur d'Alene. Its fame spread even farther when a traveling columnist for *Better Homes and Gardens* saw the garden while driving by on Highway 10. After talking to my mother, he published an article about it in that national magazine.

Mother in her renowned garden.

In reaching the high school years at thirteen, my whole viewpoint on girls changed. I had trouble adjusting to the new role of the other sex. Somehow they suddenly became more interesting, but I didn't start to date too early because I was confused about how to approach girls and my parents didn't approve of dating at that age anyway. I had started taking saxophone lessons from Mr. Fahringer in junior high school and was so scared of him I practiced hard and became quite proficient at an early age. I concentrated even more on my music to offset my other problems.

Besides, although I was very interested in girls, I was also scared to death of them. I used to go and watch the other students dancing at the matinee dances, which were held in the junior high school gym. In the first place, I didn't know how to dance, but I also didn't have the courage to try. My first love was Cathy Panabaker and I watched her hungrily from the eighth grade until well into my first year in high school. One night I worked up courage enough to ask her if I could walk her home from school and to my amazement she agreed. She lived in the Fort Sherman area, and to get to her house we had to walk through the park. I stopped her in the park and kissed her, after which she told me, "You don't kiss near as well as Kayo O'Donnel." I was humiliated and even though I took her out for rides in my canoe the next summer I didn't attempt to kiss her again.

I had also been learning to drive a car. I practiced by backing the car around our driveway and then driving it forward for a ways. In that fashion I became knowledgeable in shifting and steering, even if it was at slow speeds. Then whenever I could, I would get my mother to take me out and let me practice my driving around town. Sometimes I was able to get Bill to go with me, but that was tougher. He didn't have nearly as much patience as Mother and would punish me by pounding me on my arms with his fists, but I learned to put up with it. Despite his brutality, he was a good teacher.

When I became proficient enough, I graduated to taking my grandmother for rides. She got bored around the house and loved to go out. My parents allowed me to drive if I took her with me, so the pleasure was mutual. It gave me the opportunity to drive down through the fort grounds where there was better scenery than in my portion of town. Besides, there were a number of interesting girls, including Cathy, who lived on Military Drive. Idaho didn't require a driver's license in those days, so I was able to begin driving by myself when I was barely fourteen.

That same summer I was asked to join a group of musicians who had lined up a job to play at the Sugar Bowl during their dining hours on Sunday afternoons. This restaurant, which sold chocolate candy made on the premises and also good food, had quite a patronage of Spokane people who drove over for dinner. I was surprised at the offer and couldn't figure why they would ask me, as I had never played that type of music before. We played in a back alcove just for the patrons' listening pleasure, as there was no dancing. We were instructed not to annoy the patrons by playing too loudly. We called ourselves "The Cleff Dwellers" and must have been a smash hit. We were given one of their dinners and a small pittance for our efforts when we played. As we had just been hired for the summer, when it was over the job ceased.

That fall I began to play with the high school "Matinee Dance Orchestra" and we played not only for the school dances, but a few outside jobs as well. I remember once we even played for a Democratic rally, for which we were paid $10.00 a piece for fifteen minutes work, which wasn't bad, even though they were Democrats.

That fall we had a party at my home for the "Cleff Dwellers" to celebrate our successful summer. My folks didn't approve of my having a date, but they finally allowed me to ask Cathy. It was a real awkward setup, the orchestra played down on the first floor in the Green Room into a microphone, and there was a speaker on the third floor where we were supposed to dance. It didn't make any difference to me anyway, because I couldn't dance and was afraid to try. I don't remember what the others danced to, but some of them could dance; they were older than I. Perhaps they played records. The whole idea was really innovative though, because no one had ever heard of such a thing being done in those days.

I took Cathy for a tour of our home and I inveigled her into accompanying me to my tent, where we spent a couple of hours. Everyone wondered what had happened to us and they searched for us. Naturally it was my brother Bill who figured where we were and disturbed our tete-a-tete. It didn't make any difference anyway because I was still afraid to kiss her again. To continue my saga of Cathy, although my parents disapproved of my going to movies with a date at that age, I asked her to a movie. After much haggling they allowed me to take her provided Bill drove us there and picked us up after the movie. Big deal!! Bill felt sorry for me and arrived so late after the movie we had almost reached her home. Again **fear!** After that I gave up and never asked her out again.

Several times I have made comments about my brother Bill. Actually he was my idol, but he probably never realized it. He seemed bigger than life. He played on the football team. He was a counselor at the scout camp. He put the shot-put and made a panhandle record which held for several years. (The other men teased him about being the water boy because he was so much smaller than they were, until he was able to toss it farther than they did.) He was a big fraternity man at the University of Idaho. He swam competitively and competed against Jack Medica, an Olympic gold medal winner, able to beat him on the straight-a-way, but losing out on the turns. During the summer he would often get someone to accompany him in a boat while he swam up the lake to Three Mile Point. He played in the Idaho Pep Band, the most popular college band on the Pacific coast. (When I attended the University of Idaho for one year, I also played with them.) Finally, he even had a convertible of his own and was popular with the girls.

I didn't have the courage to ask anyone out again until my junior year in school. My attentions were forced in other directions. I practiced hard on my sax, often two and three hours a day, and spent more and more time playing in dance orchestras. Also, during the summer months I was given new jobs to do around the yard. Since it occupied a half block I took the whole week to mow the grass, trim the edges and do some weeding, doing a section each day. Of course I had to have time for going swimming and out in my canoe. By then I usually wasn't going around Tubbs Hill any longer; it was much more interesting down at the city beach because of the female companionship. Although I was afraid of girls, I loved to look at them, especially in swimming suits.

Looking back on my early years I realize there were many facets to my musical world. I had been exposed to string quartets from my earliest days, listening to my father and his friends playing on Sunday nights. As I grew older my exposure to music widened. My parents belonged to the Community Concert Series in Spokane and I often had the opportunity to listen to fine singers and instrumentalists. I especially remember the popular singer Nelson Eddy and the black baritone Paul Robeson, a much better singer, in my opinion. We also heard the renowned violinist Jascha Heifetz. The San Carlo Opera Company of San Francisco made frequent trips to Spokane on nationwide tours. Their production of Gounod's *Faust* at the State Theater was the first opera I ever heard. That may not have been the best venue for opera nor perhaps were they the finest artists, but I thoroughly enjoyed it. I was particularly impressed by the bass singer who played the part of Mephistopheles the villain.

Another musical experience I remember was the opening of the Fox Theater in Spokane. For me it seemed huge at that time. It was really a beautiful Art Deco theater, built not only for movies, but for vaudeville as well. It had a large pipe organ which would sometimes accompany the stage bands that provided music for the dancers. At first they had Fanchon and Marco productions which traveled from city to city on the west coast with changing acts. I remember the first one was a really gigantic production with maybe one hundred show girls, many of them bare breasted. They were so far away on the large stage I could hardly see anything anyway. I think the thing I remember best was when the band played a song with words that went something like "When Yuba played his tuba down in Cuba." Several years later my band played the same song; for some reason it never became a classic!

As I became more accomplished on my saxophone, I not only was playing in dance orchestras, but also the high school band and orchestra. I played everything from Sousa marches to Beethoven. Mr. Fahringer was the finest music teacher in the whole area, including Washington, and I learned many things from him. He paid great attention to detail and insisted that his musicians practice enough to achieve perfection both individually and collectively. I learned the satisfaction of doing something well with my own playing and also as a member of an organization.

In my first years with the sax I always had someone to emulate, my idol, Woody Van Fredenberg. He played both the clarinet and the sax on a level that was incomparable. No matter what I ever hoped to achieve, there was no chance I could attain his skills. He could do all sorts of impossible things on either the sax or clarinet; he knew fingerings by which he could hit higher registers on both. The books of instructions didn't show these fingerings. He could double tongue or triple tongue which were things only brass players normally were able to do. He had both a Selmer sax and clarinet. They were like owning a Rolls Royce, not for the hoi polloi. King instruments were for beginners and those in the lower echelon. Conn was for the best of high school students and the Selmer for professionals. I ultimately reached the Conn level thanks to Mr. Fahringer's skills and competition with Woody.

After my sophomore year in high school, Oliver Fuller organized an orchestra to play at the BozantaTavern and asked me to play with them. The Bozanta had originally been built by the electric rail line that ran from Spokane to Coeur d'Alene and was rather an exclusive golf club and resort on Hayden Lake. Most of the members of the club were Coeur d'Alene people, but there were Spokane members as well who had summer homes nearby. We played every Saturday night and occasionally for special parties during the week. Although neither of my parents played golf, they were members of the club for some reason.

I saw a different side of the club when I played there, as my parents didn't live that kind of a life. The members who attended the dances drank quite heavily, played the slot machines and flirted with each others' wives. I did learn from my exposure there how alcohol can change individuals from reputable business people around town to fools. It was shocking to see them playing dollar slot machines for hours at a time; it was a dollar every time they pulled the handle on the "one-armed bandit." I later learned there were some individuals who went bankrupt from excessive boozing and gambling at the Bozanta.

Normally we played from nine o'clock until midnight, but some-times a member would wish to have a private party after hours at his lake home. Then we would pack up our instruments and move to the new location. They were the wildest groups of all. The man who usually had the parties had a wife who was a little more circumspect than he. She would keep an eye on the goings on and when things got too rough, would adjourn the party by passing the hat and paying us off. We made more money for the short after-hours party than for the three hours we usually played at the Bozanta. I'm sure my mother would never have approved of my playing there if she had known what went on, but it did no lasting harm and the money was good for a fifteen-year-old kid.

A special note. Oliver Fuller, who led the band at the Tavern, later went back to school at Northwestern with my future wife and was the person who introduced us. We were both returning to school after Christmas vacation on the Northern Pacific Railroad's North Coast Limited. So something good did come out of my playing at the Tav-ern. I have always thanked my lucky star and Oliver for being lucky enough to meet Jean.

During the course of the summer I also began dating girls. It wasn't anything serious and they were all very wholesome young ladies of whom my mother approved. I would stop by their homes and flirt with them and and talk for several hours and maybe take them some-where for a soft drink. I don't remember doing much driving with them; maybe my parents wouldn't allow me to yet. Most of them were younger because the girls usually went with someone older and more experienced. At what I don't know.

In the past Mr. Sauve had caulked and repainted the canoe, but that summer he started to make me do the job under his supervision, which

The Bozanta Tavern on Hayden Lake.

Oliver Fuller's orchestra, for which I played, performed in front of this Arts and Crafts fireplace.

I continued until I left Idaho for the University of Minnesota a number of years later. I still took the canoe over to the city beach that summer, but I found more and more of the young ladies were interested in going for rides with me. Probably one of the highlights of that summer was the time when one of the very shapely young ladies slid down the metal slide into the water. The slide was dry and she was in a rubber swimming suit, which was the fad that summer. She started at the top with her suit and ended up at the bottom without it. Poor girl, she had to stay in the water until one of her friends went home and got her another suit.

I think maybe that was the summer we started going on beach parties. They were kind of a joint effort as I remember, where a group of us would get together in the planning. I don't think we even took specific dates. Someone would bring the watermelon, someone else the hot dogs and buns, some of the girls would make potato salad or cookies and we would take off for a beach by the lake. We would come in our swimming suits and build a beach fire out of wood,

A typical beach party, though a bit earlier than my high school years. The Coeur d'Alene Lumber Company and Tubbs Hill are in the background. Courtesy MNI.

Sherman Avenue much later than my childhood, but it still shows some of my favorite haunts, the Dream Theater and Harley Hudson's Missouri Kitchen.

The Sugar Bowl, where I played with the Cleff Dwellers Orchestra in 1932.

which we would scrounge around and look for. It seems there was more driftwood then than now, maybe because of the logging operations. Once the fire had burned down a bit we would cut branches to put our wieners and marshmallows on to be cooked over the coals. Along with lots of laughing and singing and swimming, we would pass a fun evening, maybe in a manner which would seem innocuous now.

During the summer Mr. Fahringer provided me with a challenge. He told me he wanted me to play the E flat clarinet in the band that fall. I had to start from scratch with it and it was horrible. I squeaked and squawked so badly my father relegated me to practicing on the third floor of the house where I wouldn't bother anyone. I didn't even like myself. It is one of the highest pitched instruments in the band, about as high as a piccolo. I did manage to play in the band in September, but I was far from good. I remember Mr. Fahringer stopped the whole band on the street one day when we were practicing and asked me to play my part solo in front of the whole world. He proved his point; I hadn't practiced hard enough and I was horrible and also humiliated. I hated the damn thing and threatened to quit the band if I had to continue playing the miserable thing. I managed to strike a bargain with him: I would continue to play in the band if he would allow me to switch to the B flat clarinet. It had a lower range and also it would help me if I could double on the clarinet in the dance orchestras. I never did like it as well as the sax, but it did help me with my orchestras.

During this period of time I started to do more things with Ged Barclay, who became a very close friend. Our fathers were both physicians who were longtime friends and associates in the Coeur d' Alene Hospital. We both played sax in the band. We both liked the lake and both had canoes. He kept his canoe on the east side of Tubbs Hill and mine was kept on the west side. Often we would arrange to meet halfway around the hill and then do things together. I guess it was from that beginning we started to see more of each other, even walking back and forth to school together. One of the things we did was to work on the engine in a boat his family had. I don't remember much about it except it was very frustrating. I don't know whether we ever got it running; seems to me it was something like the clutch slipping. We would even stay overnight at each others' homes from time to time, and I remember that winter going ice skating with Ged and Junior Potts who was a trumpet player in the band.

That fall I started to date girls more frequently and would usually take them to movies and out for some food later. Our high school hangout was the Green Lantern, a place which served soft drinks and sandwiches. Usually two or three couples would go together if we were driving, because it would depend on who could borrow their parents' car that evening. Almost none of us had cars of our own in the Depression years.

The relationship between boys and girls in those days could best be described using military terminology. There were unwritten rules and codes by which we abided. Within these boundaries there were sorties and skirmishes, with the boys advancing and the girls making strategic retreats. But in the case of a true confrontation, the boys could be counted on to withdraw in haste.

 Because there were a number of my friends who couldn't dance, we got together with some of the girls who were maybe not as popular as some of the others and lined up a dance instructor to teach us. Those were the days when we held the girls in our arms. If we were really carried away we even danced cheek to cheek with them. Depending on the speed of the music, there were three kinds of dances we learned. A drag was a slow dance in 4/4 time, a fox trot a fast dance in 2/4 time. Slowest of all and most romantic was the waltz, which was a little different step than the other two. We would practice the whole evening; step one two slide, step one two slide, and so on. While we were first learning, we danced with our instructor and later more and more with each other. In spite of playing at all the high school dances that year, I did take a date to a De Molay dance where I danced myself. (The De Molays were a boys' club sponsored by the the Masonic Lodge.)

Something happened in my junior year in high school to make all the boys in my class envious of me for the next two years. The Expates (Expatrialogus) met at my home. There was only one girls' club in the high school in Coeur d' Alene and a group of the most popular girls in school decided it was too restrictive and wished to organize a new club. They came to my mother and asked her if she would be their lay adviser. They had already asked one of the more popular teachers if she would be their faculty adviser. Mother consulted with the lay adviser to the Philomathean Club and both agreed there was probably room for two clubs in the school. The other adviser also gave Mother some suggestions as to how to best avoid some problems.

Following this, Mother told the girls she would work with them if they would agree to certain provisions. The boys were not to telephone them during the meetings. They were to stay until the meetings were over and not leave early on dates. They were to take their assignments seriously. In other words it was to enrich their lives and not be just an excuse to get out on a school night. There were other regulations which came up after they were operating. My mother enjoyed the girls, and the organization continued for many years until the school ruled out all clubs and they were forced to disband. The girls decided they wished to study foreign countries as a club goal and had trouble deciding on a name. They approached my father and he came up with the name Expatrialogus for the group. Unofficially they called themselves the Expates.

For me, it was an opportunity to meet more girls and also get in good with some of my buddies. I was supposed to be subject to the same restrictions all the boys were, but there are always means if one is clever. I didn't actually break any rules, but maybe I stretched them a little. My friends could telephone me and I could pass messages on to their girl friends. I'd go down to the kitchen by the back stairs to get a snack, when some of the girls just happened to be preparing refreshments for the group. I could tell them to pass a message on to one of the members in the other room. In the process it was an opportunity for me to get to know some of the girls better. I found their relationship with my mother helped me in my relationships even when I was at school.

My junior year I continued playing in the Matinee Dance Orchestra. Although we played for the matinee dances once a week, the Junior Prom and the Senior Ball, we received very little financial remuneration. We depended on dance jobs outside of school for most of our spending money, even though we were somewhat restricted because of our tie-in with the school.

In addition to my school work, I had my first opportunity to compete in a state contest on my saxophone. Mr. Fahringer suggested I begin to prepare for the contest during the winter. All the contestants were to play one assigned piece and an elective piece. When we had about a month to go Mr. Fahringer started telling me I wasn't practicing hard enough and Jim McKahn would be going instead of me. I just knew Jimmy wasn't that good, but I couldn't stand even the mere chance he would go in my place, so I practiced even more hours a day. I don't know why I fell for it, but Mr. Fahringer really knew how to challenge and stimulate me.

The state contests were held in Lewiston each year in April, and as the competition was not just restricted to instrumentalists, there were also various choral groups competing. Since we had a large car, my mother offered to drive, and we took several young ladies with us. (Naturally I drove the car.) After our arrival, there was some time for socializing and Lewiston was the place for it. Although it was still a little cold in Coeur d'Alene it was almost like summer in "banana belt" Lewiston. We did sneak out one evening. It was just innocent fun and helped to relax us. As it was my first competition, I was jittery because I didn't know who or what I would be competing against, maybe another Woody Van Fredenberg. Even though I didn't have the musicianship of Woody, I was so good technically no one else in Idaho could even approach my playing and I won that year.

My academic achievements in high school were less spectacular. I never was on the Honor Roll and many of the courses were a struggle for me. There were many times when I wondered why I was so dumb. Looking back on those years I now realize my major difficulty was laziness and a lack of self-confidence. I had always had trouble with arithmetic, but thanks to a an excellent teacher, I enjoyed algebra and got a decent grade. (To this day I do simple problems in arithmetic by setting up an algebraic equation.) I have to admit I flunked French twice. The reason probably was a weakness in English grammar, which I still have. I was so dumb I never thought of going to my grandmother for help. As a French Canadian, she spoke fluent French. Both years I failed to pass during the school year and made it up by being tutored the following summer by my teacher, Miss Townsend. On the other hand, I excelled in history because I enjoyed it.

Probably one of my biggest problems was a father who was too bright. If I got a B he wanted to know why I didn't get an A. If I got a C I really had a problem. Looking back on those years I realize he provided an untold amount of guidance I wasn't even aware of. However, he frequently destroyed my confidence. It was like it had been with Woody Van Fredenberg; no matter how well I did, my achievements were always clouded over when I compared myself to him.

I remember one time in English when we were memorizing stanzas from "Lady of the Lake." I had worked hard on what seemed like a large number of lines. Dad talked to me about it and then said, "Oh, yes, I remember that, I read it when I was young." He then proceeded to reel off line after line until it amounted to pages. How could I ever achieve that? The biggest criticism I have of my father was what appeared to me to be a supercilious attitude. He seemed to flaunt his intellect. It wasn't until adulthood that I began to feel as though I could measure up to my father's standards.

Years later, after graduating from dental school and graduate school, while I was practicing in Spokane, I prepared a paper for The American Academy of Pedodontics. Dad was interested in it, so I let him read it. Surprisingly, he was amazed by the depth of my knowledge and commented at great length on the scope of my efforts. I am ashamed to admit it, but I felt I had been praised by an omnipotent god.

The summer after my junior year was a continuation of the previous one. I played at the Tavern again and the summer began with parties sponsored by some of the boys' clubs from Spokane high schools. All I can say is that the girls seemed more glamorous, and their dates' clothes were better tailored and they seemed less casual than those we wore. During the intermissions I must admit we looked at the young men from Spokane with some envy.

My brother's car "Virtue" deserves special mention. It was a 1929 Oldsmobile convertible roadster with a rumble seat. Although of a bilious color sort of like a clay pot, it was a wonderful car with many appurtenances including a canvas top, a radiator cap, wire spoke wheels and two spare tires in fender wells which ran into running boards. It also had a spotlight on the driver's side and side shields which attached to the windshield. The car was racy in the summer when the top was folded back and cold in the winter. After Bill went back to medical school in Ohio I was able to persuade my parents to let me use his car. Ged Barclay and I had discovered "derby hats," which had been the style many years before and were no longer worn in this country. To distinguish us from the common horde, we used to wear the hats everywhere we went. We would cruise the town in these hats as we drove down the street with the top down.

My brother Bill's Oldsmobile roadster "Virtue." I got to use it after Bill left for medical school.

We also delighted in going hunting with the spotlight at night down in the fort grounds along the river bank, where young people would go to neck. One night when my brother was home from college, we went on one of our excursions. He had borrowed Mother's big Buick that night and we caught him down along the river. For some reason he objected to our turning the spotlight on him and started to chase us all over town: up and down streets, in and out of alleys, until finally we hit a bump coming out an alley and the windshield came crashing down and broke. (It could be tipped up and down.) You can bet with the accumulation of misdemeanors that night, Bill was not too happy with me. I of course had to pay to replace the windshield and I also received a very stern lecture from him. (I was too big for him to hit me on the arm any longer.)

Even in my day young men sometimes did wild irrational things. There were several episodes which come to my mind. One was in the winter and happened after Ged and I had been out to Fernan Lake skating. For some reason we drove down East Lakeshore Drive, which is right on the lake. As we were driving down the street, suddenly in the middle of one block we felt we wanted to turn around. I drove over the sidewalk and made a U turn on one of the lawns (the ground was frozen solid so I was sure the lawn wouldn't be damaged) and then proceeded back the other direction. (There was no curb.) Unbeknown to us a couple further down the street were out for a walk and saw us. They phoned the police when they got home and reported us, even lying and saying we had almost run over them. *We were at least a half a block away from them, but the fact they were the wealthiest and most influential couple in town didn't help our credibility.* This of course had its repercussions when the police phoned my father to ask him who had been driving the car. The police and my father came to an understanding with my being forbidden to drive for a month, which actually was convenient for my parents, as they were going to be out of town for about three weeks and wanted some excuse for me not to drive while they were gone.

When my parents left, they had my Aunt Mary stay at our house to keep an eye on me. This worked out well, as Ged's parents were out of town also and we took turns staying at each house. His parents had left one car at home which Ged was free to use, but that wasn't enough for us, as it was a roadster and didn't have room for our girl-friends. Being true rapscallions, we solved our difficulty in a very honorable way. We would push the car out the rear door of the barn onto the back street and start it up and drive off. Of course I was pledged not to drive, so naturally Ged drove, which left me in the back seat with my girlfriend. Tough! Another irresponsible event was one day late in June, when I had driven down to the city beach in Virtue. Our group, which included not only Ged and Junior, but also the owner of the Silver Grill Restaurant in town, had been getting together every afternoon and had often joked about swimming in four lakes in one day. We decided this was the day, so we all went up and piled into the car, some in the rumble seat, some in front. We took off for Liberty Lake on a paved road for our first swim and then cross-country to Newman Lake. After that swim we careened off on graveled roads to Hayden, our fourth lake. The ride was wild, we hung onto the car while changing clothes as we speeded along at over 70 miles per hour, Virtue's top speed, singing bawdy songs. Fortu-nately, there were not so many cars on the road in those days and we survived.

Coeur d' Alene High School, which I attended as well as several members of my family.

My senior year began with a bang or maybe I should say a sour note. Mr. Fahringer selected me to direct the Matinee Dance Orchestra that year, but I began with severe handicaps. In my sophomore year I had been the only one who *had not* played in the orchestra before; this year I was the only one who *had* played in it before. The initial difficulty was that I was plagued with a drummer who couldn't hold a beat. My friend Ged was one of the sax players and was a natural with jazz. The other sax, despite his lack of experience, learned to play well. One of the trumpet players had a brother who was an excellent jazz player and he must have learned from him. The other one was too young and immature to do very well. The violinist was pretty. I would rather have had a bass viol than a sousaphone, but I learned how to adapt to it. The piano player was the best one of all. She had played with orchestras before and knew the jazz idiom. It sounds like a rather pitiful group, but they turned out better than I anticipated. I had the drummer use a metronome when we practiced so he could learn how to hold a beat and also have some idea about tempo. The others improved with enough rehearsals and home practice.

After several months we really had a pretty good group. In fact when Miss Townsend approached Mr. Fahringer about forming a small orchestra to accompany singers who were putting on Gilbert and Sullivan's *H.M.S. Pinafore*, he suggested my orchestra. As it turned out we added several more musicians to the group. We were quite versatile and did a creditable job as a theater orchestra.

Because of frequent visits to his office for passes to go down town to buy music, I developed a rapport with both Mr. Campbell, the principal, and his secretary. Finally, he selected me for the job of supervising the hall patrol. Mr. Campbell was a former marine and believed in discipline. If anyone left class, a pass was required, so students wouldn't just be roaming the hall at will. There were monitors on each floor and anyone out of their room had to present their pass to a monitor to record their time in and out. For my own period as a monitor I selected the last one, when I was supposed to have study hall.

A lot of my time was spent visiting with both the principal and his secretary; in fact they even sent me to the little store across the street to buy candy bars. The secretary and I became so friendly before the year was over I even dated her discreetly. With her position, it wouldn't do for anyone to know she dated a student. I was able to get out of school almost anytime I wanted though, even for occasional trips to Spokane to purchase music.

Despite my friendship with the principal, I still wasn't above pranks from time to time. One escapade I plotted for some time. I came across a cannon firecracker from the previous Fourth and set up a deal with my two friends whom I had appointed as monitors the last period. At each end of the high school we had stairwells which ran from the basement to the second floor. They were open so it played into my scheme. My friend Dick Fischer was on the second floor, I was on the first floor, and another buddy was in the basement level. I went into the principal's office and was talking to his secretary while my friend in the basement arranged to be at the north end of the building. Dick went to the south end of the building and at a prearranged time lit the firecracker and dropped it down into the stairwell so it exploded in the basement. Everyone was studying; it was very quiet and suddenly this tremendous **Bang!** The sound reverberated through the basement, swelled as it rose and echoed up and down the halls. Suddenly doors burst open and teachers and students erupted from their rooms in panic. It was bedlam! It was the end of classes for that day as everyone clustered around in little knots talking. I suspect Mr. Campbell knew who was the instigator. His eyes twinkled later when the subject was brought up, but he never said a word.

By then I was trying to make up for my past timidity with the fairer sex. Ged and I would double date, he going with the piano player in the orchestra and I playing the field. Although I went to several dances during the year, I still wasn't confident with my dancing. Usually we went to movies. I remember how much I wanted to dance like Fred Astaire and of course I was in love with Ginger Rogers. It was a far cry from my earlier cowboy movies.

I became more and more impressed with myself that year. My school work was going well. The dating was going well. I was a big shot with the principal. I entered the state contest on my sax and won again. I had lots of friends because of the Expates meeting at my home and my friends who got monitor jobs.

Something very special happened just before school was out. The whole high school band and orchestra came up to our home for hot dogs, hamburgers and baked beans. I don't remember how many there were, but it was well over a hundred and was the largest group ever in our back yard. After dinner we played a concert for my parents. I had a role in our graduation ceremonies also. On Class Day the Matinee Orchestra played selected music. For the commencement exercises I played a saxophone solo. It was May 22, 1935 and I was a week short of seventeen. With all the things I did my senior year in high school I don't think I ever again felt so important as I did that year. My good friend Ged Barclay jokingly called me "Destiny's Tot." I think I believed him. But a great deal had gone into my destiny before I reached my high school graduation. I was the product, good or bad, of two loving parents. I was proud to be the son of both of them. My father was the biggest man in any gathering in every way; my mother, the prettiest and youngest woman. My father was responsible for much of the culture and direction in my growth but had little time to give to me personally. He was too busy being a general practicing physician when it was a twenty-four-hour a day job. They made house calls in those days.

My mother gave me her constant love and provided the companionship a growing boy needed. It was her responsibility, along with Mr. Fahringer's, to see that I practiced. She accompanied me to the football and basketball games and helped cheer my teams on to victory. If the band needed transportation to an out-of-town game she drove a carload of musicians. In my early years she was even responsible for my disciplining, although one piercing look from my father's dark brown eyes had more impact than other forms of punishment. My formative years also owe a great deal to several fine teachers already mentioned and to friends, some gone, and others whom I enjoy to this day.

Finally, I was extremely lucky to grow up where I did. Coeur d'Alene and its surroundings in which I roamed became a part of me. The town, the lake and the woods provided endless scope for discovery and adventure. Furthermore, my childhood took place during a time when children *could* roam freely. Although my youth had its share of sorrow and trauma, it seems to have come as close to the ideal as possible, a wonderful combination of freedom and structure.

My brother Bill, Mother and I while I was still in high school.